# THE EMPLOYERS'
# HANDBOOK TO 401(k)
# SAVINGS PLANS

# THE EMPLOYERS' HANDBOOK TO 401(k) SAVINGS PLANS

*Christian D. Rahaim*

iUniverse, Inc.
New York   Lincoln   Shanghai

# THE EMPLOYERS' HANDBOOK TO 401(k) SAVINGS PLANS

iUniverse books may be ordered through booksellers or by contacting:

iUniverse
2021 Pine Lake Road, Suite 100
Lincoln, NE 68512
www.iuniverse.com
1-800-Authors (1-800-288-4677)


ISBN: 0-595-33630-2 (Pbk)
ISBN: 0-595-66982-4 (Cloth)

Printed in the United States of America

# CONTENTS

# PREFACE

During author Chris Rahaim's twelve years in human resource management he has dismantled and terminated the company benefit structure and plans of the nation's most complex bankruptcy, spearheaded complex mergers and acquisitions, conducted due diligence for government investigations and mergers, acquisitions and divestitures.

The author received his law degree from Loyola University, a master's degree in Business Administration from the University of Mississippi, and a bachelor's degree in Psychology from the University of Mississippi. Author of numerous articles (including "ERISA, OWBPA, & WARN: The Bermuda Triangle of Employment Severance Agreements," "The Doctrine of Respondeat Superior Applied to Electronic Communications," "The Effect of Mandatory Pre-dispute ADR Agreements on Title VII Claims," "Comparison of Cognitive Ability Test and Clinical Assessment on Employment Selection," "The Success of Skill-Based Pay in Achieving Goals"), he has negotiated agreements and settlements with the U.S. Department of Labor, Pension Benefit Guaranty Corporation, and the Internal Revenue Service. Additionally, working with and providing information to the U.S. Senate and U.S. House of Representatives on pension legislation provides the author exhaustive insight apropos savings plans in the workplace.

*The Employers' Handbook to 401(k) Savings Plans* contains essential material, culminating in an informative and compelling body of work. From the growth and development of the 401(k) plan to its future in the workplace, the author provides captive inclinations that keep the reader engaged with clear, concise, and trustworthy manner. Throughout this book, the chapters build the necessary framework for the reader to develop an understanding of the content, operations, and issues with operating a 401(k) savings plan in today's volatile environment.

This publication is designed to provide accurate and authoritative information concerning the subject matter covered. It is sold with the understanding that the author is not engaged in rendering legal, investment, or other professional service herein. If legal, investment, accounting advice or other expert assistance is required, competent professional person should be sought. The information contained herein represents the views of the author and is not intended to represent legal or investment advice by the author. Furthermore, it is not intended to establish an express or implied attorney-client relationship.

# Chapter 1—OVERVIEW OF 401(k) SAVINGS PLANS

The numbers tell the story. The increase in 401(k) assets during the last decade accounts for the most explosive growth among all qualified benefit and retirement plans. In fact, from 1992 through 2003, 401(k) assets grew from $410 billion to $2.2 trillion[1], which is roughly 20 percent growth per year (compounded).

Although 401(k) asset growth over the past ten years has occurred mostly among larger plans, currently, and going forward, the new entrants of this market will be primarily from smaller company plans. The growth shift is attributable to the fact that large and midsize plans are growing primarily through ongoing contributions and appreciation, rather than through the formation of new plans. Penetration of this market is as high as 94 percent for plans with more than 5,000 participants.

On the other hand, the small-plan market has considerable room for expansion. Moreover, although this market has roughly $280 billion in assets today, growth estimates place assets at more than a 40 percent growth per year (compounded) over the next five years. In addition, that amount of available 401(k) assets will continue to fuel tremendous competition among service providers.

During the 1990s, many providers tried to capture a slice of the 401(k) business; however, there were simply too many competitors to be sustained by this marketplace. With the evolution of technology and tremendous growth of both assets and participants, today eight providers account for over 50 percent of the 401(k) business. The shakeout in the industry that resulted in such a consolidation was the providers' ability to react to rapidly changing landscape in this business. Size, resources, and the ability to provide low-cost services gave 401(k) providers a competitive advantage. Single-provider, bundled services became essential because unbundled arrangements typically cannot compete from a cost standpoint and ease of administration. Additional competitive factors included the ability to offer a range of investment styles and make capital investments in new technology to provide "on-demand" information to participants through the Internet.

---

1    U.S. Department of Labor data.

Today, the driving factors have shifted beyond basic record-keeping services on the Internet to include investment education and advice, dynamic retirement modeling, asset allocation, push emails, and other automated services. Moreover, the market will be dominated by those providers that not only satisfy the technology requirements, but can offer an open architecture investment platforms and fiduciary services.

# 401(k) POPULARITY

The starting place of the 401(k) market's shift during the last decade accounts for the numerous service providers currently vying for any particular piece of the business. Essentially the growth in these plans has been self-perpetuating. As investment management organizations recognized the appeal of this market for their services, they did a lot to promote plans to employers who had not yet established them. This growing number of new plans resulted in extraordinary growth in annual 401(k) plan contributions. The increase in contributions attracted new entrants to the market who will continue to convince other employers to create new plans. Other factors contributing to the universal success of 401(k) plans include the following:

- The general desire of employees to save money on a pretax basis
- Employer-sponsor dissatisfaction with the regulatory and administrative burdens of defined-benefit plans (traditional pension plans wherein the employer guarantees a specified benefit to be paid in the future and must fund accordingly) as well as their costs
- The portability of defined-contribution plans (plans in which the employer promises to make a current contribution rather than a future benefit payment)

## Industry Shifts

Whatever the bona fide factors contributing to the success of 401(k) plans may be, it is clear that these plans have become the dominant retirement funding vehicle for a multitude of employers. The expectations, however, are shifting. Although the goal of making intelligent savings and investment decisions for retirement continues for participants, their methods are much more sophisticated than previous. Today, participants demand an open architecture investment platform, maximum portability, education advice, and lower fees. On the other hand, employers attempt to balance the desires of participants with their needs for reduced administration, maximum value (a cost-benefit ratio), and managed fiduciary responsibilities.

Looking into the future, although the greatest number of new plans will be created by smaller companies, larger plans are restructuring and reexamining their service providers in light of the competitive pressures to: (1) provide broad investment options, (2) manage fiduciary duties, and (3) maximize value.

## Forces Influencing the Future of the Industry

The success of the 401(k) plan marketplace today has largely been shaped by a combination of marketing and technological innovation. 401(k) marketers have done an impressive job of tapping into the collective consciousness of the American worker. More than ever before, people are beginning to understand the need to save and are doing so in their 401(k) plans. 401(k) has become synonymous with savings and United States workers are becoming savers. As workers see their balances grow and continue to learn that they are on their own in terms of funding their own retirement, workers will increase their rates of savings within 401(k) plans. This will continue to shape the future growth of the 401(k) plan market.

In addition to marketing influences, technological enhancements will have great impact on the future of the market. Although technological innovation eases the administrative process, it also brings both investment power and information to the individual participants. Because the marketplace has become so competitive, the most successful future 401(k) plan service providers will be those who can provide state-of-the-art administrative and participant communications systems at competitive prices. Further, given that future growth in this market will occur in smaller companies, service providers must be committed to developing technology for small-plan sponsors.

Nevertheless, technology is not the only force driving the future in the marketplace. Plan sponsors have become increasingly aware of the scope and nature of their fiduciary responsibilities under the Employee Retirement Income Security Act (ERISA). Myriads of unanswered legal questions pertain to plan fiduciaries' obligations and potential liability within 401(k) plans. Additionally, these issues are under heightened scrutiny from both civil litigation and government investigations.

The U.S. Department of Labor's section 404(c) regulations and delineation of investment education versus advice has added fuel to the debate, rather than settling it. These regulations raise all sorts of issues that must be answered over time. The regulations illustrate the complexity of the issues involved when investment control is given to plan participants. Thus, future plan sponsors are likely to focus more on whether competing 401(k) service providers can help them understand and manage their responsibilities under ERISA.

Recently, the three factors most closely related to fiduciary responsibility are asset management, plan fees, and participant communications. Asset management refers to the investment process in a 401(k) plan. Plan fees refer to those fees necessary to operate the plan and paid for with plan assets. Participant communications refers to educating and informing participants about the features and options in the plan. In the early years of 401(k) plans, sponsors focused their attention more on the administrative or record-keeping component of the plan than on asset management and participant communications. Undoubtedly, as we will explore later, their focus is changing.

Investment management relative to plan objectives has become a central issue in the selection of 401(k) service providers. Flexibility of investment management has also driven this process, as plan sponsors insist more and more on broadening their investment option ranges to suit the needs of their participants.

Plan expenses charged against plan assets has become the recent focus of the U.S. Department of Labor (DOL) and Internal Revenue Service (IRS). Promulgated by increasing participant apprehension regarding understandable disclosure of fees, plan expenses has been an issue. Questions about these central areas of concern are as follows: is the fee an expense of the plan, is it reasonable, and is it properly allocated? Moreover, the plan expenses that are charged must be disclosed to participants.

Finally, the enormous demand for effective participant communications will be a significant force shaping the 401(k) market. The requirement that participants receive sufficient information in order to make informed investment decisions will cause the best competitors to develop innovative communications programs. Targeted, effective communications programs have become imperative to address the plan sponsor's potential liability associated with participant-directed plans. Both the regulatory and practical issues are covered in detail in Chapter 10.

## DEFINING A 401(k) PLAN

Market demands, civil litigation, and regulatory changes have dramatically influenced the growth and development of 401(k) plans. The chapters that follow offer a detailed discussion of each component of the 401(k) plan and what future developments might be expected. First, it is important to have a clear understanding of a 401(k) plan's basic features to truly get a sense for the plan's ongoing evolution.

A 401(k) plan is a qualified retirement plan that is a cash or deferred arrangement under which a covered employee can elect to have a portion of his or her compensation (otherwise payable in cash) contributed as a pretax reduction in salary (however, some plans also accept after-tax contributions from employees).

# Figure 1-1: Relationship between a Qualified Retirement Plan and a 401(k) Savings Plan

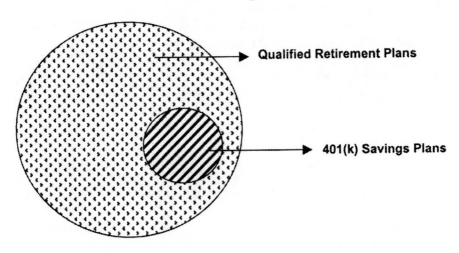

Qualified Retirement Plans

401(k) Savings Plans

Assets are invested in stocks, bonds, guaranteed investment contracts (GICs), cash-equivalents, or a diversified portfolio of these investments. At the end of 2003, participant accounts where invested as follows.

## Figure 1-2: Allocation of Plan Assets

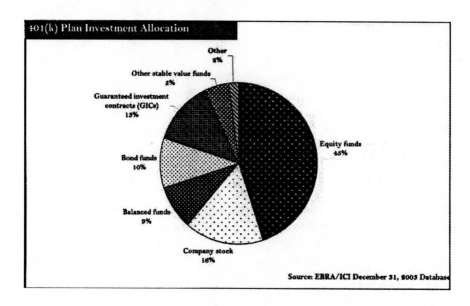

The pretax contributions as well as earnings on an account are taxed only when withdrawn. Employers generally have the discretion whether or not to make matching contributions to their workers' 401(k) plan. 401(k) plans are subject to considerable regulatory oversight by federal agencies because they are "qualified" employee benefit plans. In general, the two primary laws that govern 401(k) Savings Plans are the Internal Revenue Code of 1986 (or the "Code") and the Employee Retirement Income Security Act of 1974 (or "ERISA"). The many features of 401(k) plans include those described in the following sections.

## Employee Contributions

Very simply, a 401(k) plan is a tax-advantaged employee savings plan. Employees whose companies sponsor such plans are able to save money directly from their paycheck before any taxes are taken. Accordingly, they can participate in a disciplined, long-term savings plan while avoiding taxes on the money they contribute to the plan until a later date.

In addition to pretax contributions, some 401(k) plans allow employees to make after-tax or voluntary contributions. These after-tax contributions may accumulate tax-deferred without all of the restrictions on distributions that apply to pretax contributions.

## Optional Employer Contributions

One of the most attractive features of a 401(k) plan is the employer contribution, or company match. Employer contributions benefit those employees who choose to participate in the plan. For every dollar employees save in the plan, their employer may provide a matching contribution, typically based on a percentage of the employee's own contribution. Although these matching contributions are optional, more than 75 percent of all 401(k) plan sponsors make employer contributions to the plan.[2] Matching contributions are covered in Chapter 3.

## Employee Investment Direction

Participant control over individual investment decisions is one of the most distinctive features of a 401(k) plan. Referred to as participant-directed plans, 401(k) plans allow participants to choose the investments for their retirement savings and are subject to substantial regulation by the DOL, as discussed in Chapter 7.

---

2    Plansponsor.com, 2003 DC Survey.

In a participant-directed plan, employees typically are given a selection of roughly two to six investment options among which they may allocate their savings. Employees in participant-directed plans also have the ability to adjust their investment selections periodically, as infrequently as semiannually to as frequently and more commonly as daily.

In more unique situations, the employer does not offer any preset range of options, and employees may invest their money in virtually any available investment vehicle. As a practical matter, these latter plans are administratively difficult, because there is no viable way to perform plan-level reports. Further, from a fiduciary management perspective, such plans provide no opportunity for plan oversight.

Both types of plans should be distinguished from so-called employer-directed plans, in which the employee has no power to select among investment options. In such circumstances, designated people in the sponsoring organization serve as "fiduciaries," which have responsibility for selecting the investments or investment advisory organizations to manage the plan's assets. In such cases, all employees' contributions are pooled and managed as a single portfolio. As a result, all employees have the same investment experience regardless of their individual circumstances.

## Distribution Restrictions

Distributions from 401(k) plans are subject to the Internal Revenue Code's rules for qualified plan distributions. Most plans provide for distribution in a lump sum at termination of employment. Section 401(k) plans also permit employees, in some instances, to make withdrawals even though the employees are still employed by the plan sponsor. Such withdrawals are either in the form of so-called hardship withdrawals or participant loans.

# HISTORICAL PERSPECTIVE ON 401(k) PLANS

To fully understand where the 401(k) marketplace is headed, it helps to get a sense of where it has been. Created by the sweeping enactment of the Tax Reform Act of 1978, which included a provision that became Internal Revenue Code (Code) Sec. 401(k) for which the plans are named, under which employees are not taxed on the portion of income they elect to receive as deferred compensation rather than as direct cash payments.

Before 1978, deferred compensation arrangements ("cash or deferred arrangements," known as CODAs), which allowed some compensation and resulting tax liability to be deferred, predate 401(k) plans by several decades and are viewed as their precursors. An ongoing debate between employers and the IRS about the extent of restrictions on such plans culminated in IRS guidance in 1956,[3] which was revised seven years later in response to a federal court ruling (*Hicks v. U.S.*) on the deferral of profit-sharing contributions.[4]

The Employee Retirement Income Security Act of 1974 (ERISA) banned the issuance of Treasury regulations before 1977 that would affect plans in place on June 27, 1974, thereby freezing a regulation proposed by the IRS in December 1972 that would have severely restricted the tax-deferred status of such plans. This feat restricted the creation of new plans. After Congress extended the moratorium deadline twice, the IRS withdrew the proposed regulation in 1978. ERISA also mandated a study of salary reduction plans that influenced 1978 legislation creating 401(k) plans. The Revenue Act of 1978 added permanent provisions to the IRC, sanctioning the use of salary reductions as a source of plan contributions. The law went into effect on January 1, 1980.

Actually, the authority and intent of Congress to create a vehicle of such magnitude are not clear. Indeed, a review of the legislative record suggests that Congress inadvertently granted employers the authority to establish such plans. Moreover, an examination of the facts surrounding the first-ever 401(k) plan application reviewed by the IRS supports the view that Congress had not intended to create a vehicle that would result in such vast changes in the landscape of employee benefit plans.

In 1981, a benefits consultant named Ted Benna received formal sanction from the IRS for his novel plan design based on the new 401(k) section of the Code.[5] The Revenue Act of 1978 had added this section of the Code. Benna wanted to offer features that are familiar to most plans today, but were innovative at the time—pretax salary reduction, company matching contributions, and higher participation rates from the rank-and-file employees—in addition to customary Social Security benefits. Benna realized early that the tax savings alone would not offer enough incentive for many employees to participate in the plan, so he included in his plan design matching contributions from the employer, similar to the feature of an employer-directed plan. He named his packaged product a cash-op.

At this time, the concept of employee retirement savings was attractive. President Reagan had been stressing the need to encourage personal saving through tax-deferred individual retirement accounts (IRAs). Payroll deduction IRAs were allowed in 1981.

---

3    Rev. Rul, 56-497.
4    Rev. Rul. 63-180.
5    Ted Benna, The Day I Designed The First 401(K) Savings Plan.

Nearly everyone Benna approached with this novel idea was skeptical, including several large insurance companies. However, Benna and his partner Ed Johnson spoke to officials at the U.S. Treasury Department and were advised that Benna's interpretation of the Code was correct. The IRS approved Benna's plan provisionally in the spring of 1981, while continuing to work on the 401(k) regulations.

Benna's design was an entirely new approach, clearly not intended by the legislation. It took the IRS until late 1981 to issue the first proposed 401(k) regulations, which in effect gave the Johnson Companies' plan official endorsement. In February 1982, the IRS announced that taxpayers could rely on the proposed regulations until final regulations were published. In essence, the IRS regulations proposed in 1982 specifically recognized that a qualified cash or deferred arrangement may take the form of a salary reduction agreement. This mark of approval by the IRS opened the doors to 401(k) plans nationally.

Benna's original application created the first qualified employee tax-deferred savings plan. The statutory and regulatory sections authorizing this investment plan occurred under section 401(k) of the Internal Revenue Code, hence the name 401(k) plan.

In essence, 401(k) plans are nothing more than a method for employees to save money before they pay income taxes. In spite of that, this relatively simple concept has generated a new era in employee benefit plan design, litigation, compliance, administration, and investment management. No one could have predicted the level of growth and popularity of 401(k) plans when the IRS received its first 401(k) plan application in 1981.

# Chapter 2—COMPONENTS OF 401(k) PLANS

Considering a 401(k) plan's complexity, plan sponsors have always looked for service solutions that can effectively integrate their plan's multiple components. Therefore, sponsors found the prospect of obtaining all plan services from a single provider to be extremely appealing. Perceptive marketers, recognizing the growth potential of this market, seized the opportunity to promote "one-stop shopping" plan services. Unfortunately for plan sponsors, many providers failed to deliver on the simplicity and efficiency promised in the marketing literature.

Of the providers unable to deliver on their promises, most offered a loosely-connected arrangement of independent service providers. Marketing packages and salespeople began to tout these 401(k) programs as bundled plans, containing everything a plan sponsor would need. Yet, as many plan sponsors soon discovered, the term bundled was being used to apply to virtually every plan on the market, including plans that were not bundled in a way that would provide efficiencies to the plan sponsor. In many cases, the electronic links among the so-called bundled providers were far too tenuous to maintain accuracy and effective plan administration, the hallmarks of a bundled plan. The promise of simplicity by these service providers gave way to the reality that administering 401(k) plans requires more than a facade, especially given the intricate nature of regulatory and reporting requirements. In addition, the image of the bundled plan was demeaned in the process, almost relegated to industry jargon with no real meaning.

This situation needs to be distinguished from the case of a truly bundled plan in which advanced technology and service platforms allow a single entity or group of entities to provide a complete package of investment, trustee, participant record keeping, and communication services. A truly bundled plan provides enormous convenience to the plan sponsor and participants because of superior service capabilities. As they make the step into offering employees this benefit, plan sponsors need to know how to differentiate between fact and fiction for bundled plans. This distinction is examined in Chapter 6.

The demands of the marketplace have pushed the 401(k) plan to the outer limits of record-keeping capabilities, transforming it into a transactional participant account, with complexities beyond even the individual brokerage or mutual fund account. Not surprisingly, most of the success stories with respect to providing single-provider bundled services occurred among the larger mutual fund companies that already had experience with this type of transactional account and related service. The most successful 401(k) service providers today provide all necessary services under one roof.

Other early promises focused on the methods and content of employee communications regarding 401(k) plans. Buzzwords and industry jargon were a poor substitute for content, causing participants to jeopardize their future by making ineffective long-term investment allocations. 401(k) plan participants showed extremely risk-averse behavior with respect to their investments because they had little investment sophistication and simply did not understand the benefits of asset allocation. In fact, most participants invested heavily in Guaranteed Investment Contracts (GICs) and fixed-income investments with no inflation protection in their portfolios. As manifest in Chapter 10's discussion of participant communications, education has made great strides, evidenced by a more appropriate allocation in participant accounts.

Finally, some early 401(k) providers suggested that the transfer of investment responsibility to individual plan participants would absolve the plan sponsors of all potential liability associated with investment performance in participants' accounts.[6] However, plan sponsors now realize the magnitude of their fiduciary responsibilities with respect to these plans and are taking measures to adequately fulfill them.

## THE COMPONENTS OF THE 401(k) PLAN

Anyone familiar with 401(k) plans might characterize them as an intricate relationship between the following component services: investment management, participant record keeping, plan administration, and participant communications. Each component by itself is equally important and, ideally, should be well coordinated with the other plan components.

---

6    See In re Unisys Sav. Plan Lititg., 173 F.3d 145 (3d Cir. 1999).

Figure 2-1: 401(k) Plan Components

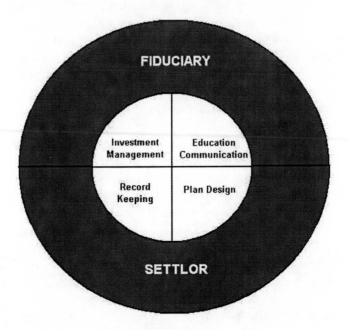

Prospective sponsors of new 401(k) plans often make the mistake of viewing the plan as though it were a simple entity, rather than a product of the complex relationship between component services. An effectively bundled program can make the plan simple to the plan sponsor and participants, but what is behind the scenes is somewhat complex.

# TAKING A CLOSER LOOK AT THE COMPONENTS

## Investments

Most 401(k) plans today enable participants to select among a series of professionally managed portfolios. By offering a range of investment options, these plans allow participants to construct their own portfolios, depending on their individual circumstances. Participants normally have the ability periodically to make changes in their investment mixes (allocation), most commonly on a daily basis.

Although ERISA requires that plan fiduciaries exercise considerable prudence in the selection and maintenance of plan investment options, early on in the creation of these plans many sponsors did not focus enough attention on their plan's investment component. As a result, many 401(k) plans offered a limited range of options that did not necessarily give their participants the opportunity to practice effective asset allocation.

Today, plan sponsors are focusing more on the investment or asset management component of their plans, such that they are adding investment options and more carefully considering the investment needs of their particular participant population. In addition, sponsors are recognizing the need for written investment policies to provide guidance and standards in both the selection and monitoring of the plan's investment options, often relying upon consultants or investment professionals for the development of these standards.

## Participant Record Keeping

One of the most rapidly evolving components of a 401(k) plan—participant record keeping—is the process of maintaining participants' account balances and records in the plan. Such activities include, but are not limited to, facilitating fund transfers, valuing participant accounts, and reconciling all records on specified dates.

Much of the enormous development in participant record keeping has been driven by demand for daily record-keeping systems that mandate sophisticated links among all plan components. As a result, the number one priority among industry service providers is systems development and technological innovation to ensure accuracy and timely execution of transaction processing. Increasingly, both participants and plan sponsors require on-demand information, which can only be provided through a daily system.

Along with the move toward such daily systems has come a move away from unbundled record-keeping services. The problem with unbundled services (and services that call themselves bundled and are really unbundled) is that the investment manager, the record keeper, the plan sponsor, and the participants all need to communicate with each other. Yet, unbundled arrangements lack the technology to link all of these components together efficiently. Because many of these systems do not have true electronic interfaces at every level, they rely heavily on cumbersome manual processing, resulting in delays and inaccuracies. As such, the ability to execute transactions and provide information essentially at "warp" speed simply does not exist in an unbundled service arrangement. And, in addition to the inherent servicing inefficiencies in this type of arrangement, unbundled services cannot compete with single provider bundled services from a cost or service perspective. Ultimately, competitive pressures will cause the demise of many traditional unbundled 401(k) service providers, except for very large asset based plans.

## Plan Consulting

Part of the plan administration function, and a very important aspect of a bundled service arrangement, is plan consulting. Whereas service providers should offer several prototype plan options, there are still complex design and regulatory issues relating to everything from control groups to multiple-use limitations. The service provider must offer plan consulting and design support because these extremely complex issues may have a different impact on each individual plan.

## Participant Communications

Rapidly becoming the central focus for most plan sponsors, participant communications are paramount to the success of a 401(k) plan. Participant communications generally refer to the responsibility to educate all who participate in the plan about the plan's features and investment options. Therefore, the plan needs to support the participants' efforts through an effective education program because 401(k) plans allow participants to contribute their own money and (in most instances) to make their own investment decisions.

In the past, participant communications have been largely inadequate, because they were approached as a one-time event at enrollment rather than an ongoing process. Accordingly, participants were overwhelmed with information when they first joined the plan, and learned little or nothing about how to direct and redirect their investments in a way that best suited their own needs. Essentially, they were unprepared to manage their retirement investments over the long term, which jeopardized their future financial security.

Today, plan sponsors realize that if they give participants control over investments, sponsors also must give them the tools necessary to make informed investment decisions. Much emphasis has been placed on developing strategic, long-term education programs that help participants become more informed investors, while allowing plan sponsors to limit the risk of fiduciary liability. Types and content of participant communications are covered at length in Chapter 10.

## Legal Components

Another significant aspect of 401(k) plans is the legal or regulatory component. 401(k) plans are governed by a multitude of regulations by both the Internal Revenue Service (IRS) and the U.S. Department of Labor (DOL).

In very general terms, the IRS regulations governing 401(k) plans ensure that the plan operates fairly with respect to all employees, rather than as a mechanism to reward senior persons within the organization. To this end, the 401(k) regulations impose many tests generally designed to maintain an IRS-acceptable balance as to the extent to which all classes of employees participate and benefit under the plan. In essence, the 401(k) regulations preclude a company from operating a plan that discriminates in favor of a class of staff called "highly compensated employees."[7] The IRS ensures compliance by threatening plan disqualification, which effectively means taxation and penalties.

The DOL has the authority and responsibility under ERISA to govern the investment management of qualified plan assets in order to protect the interest of participants and beneficiaries. To do so, the DOL must regulate the investments in the plan as well as the people who manage plan assets and operations—the plan fiduciaries. All of the DOL's enforcement tools are designed to ensure that the plan is managed prudently.

Currently, the regulatory issue most applicable to 401(k) plans is section 404(c), whose regulations govern participant-directed plans. Although these regulations are discussed extensively throughout this book, it is important to note that these regulations are simply part of a greater regulatory scheme under ERISA. These regulations have considerable impact on the fiduciaries' responsibilities in managing the plan investment and communications process.

In sum, the combined regulatory efforts of both the IRS and DOL contribute to the complexity of the 401(k) plan itself. Understanding the legal and regulatory principles that form the basis of this regulatory framework is essential in order for plan sponsors and their advisors to effectively manage the plan and the associated risks.

---

7   Treas. Reg. §1.401(a)(4).

# Chapter 3—DESIGNING AND ESTABLISHING A 401(k) PLAN

The purpose of this chapter is to highlight some of the major issues a prospective 401(k) plan sponsor must address in designing and installing a new plan. It should be noted that this chapter is not intended to be exhaustive on the complexities involved in plan design and operation, and that new plan sponsors are strongly encouraged to seek professional advice from qualified professionals in the design and operational phases of their plans.

## DESIGNING THE PLAN

Plan design is the process of determining the options and elements that will be incorporated into the plan. In the early years of 401(k) plans, this process tended to be rather time consuming because the 401(k) regulations had not yet been promulgated and practitioners were essentially relying on interpretations and common practices. At that time, there was also a greater element of creativity and experimentation with respect to the types of plan options or attributes the IRS would approve in its approval process.

Today, many of these issues have been resolved, so that a qualified plan advisor can predict with some level of certainty what design options will meet with IRS approval and, as a practical matter, will make the plan work. Despite the relative certainty about IRS positioning, through, the design process should not be oversimplified, nor should it be ignored. The extra time spent in the early stages of the plan design process can dictate whether the plan ultimately is successful.

The design decisions relate to everything from eligibility to matching contribution formulas. Virtually all design decisions can have an impact on the employees' perception of the plan as well as the ability of the plan to satisfy the plan regulatory requirements. Thus, each element should be carefully considered so that the sponsor can predict the effect that such options will have on the employees and or the plan's ability to satisfy the myriad legal and regulatory tests within the 401(k) plan regulations.

Just as the contractor needs a good plan to build a solid house, the plan sponsor needs to take the time in advance to design the plan's features to ensure its success. In doing this, there is a great temptation to rely on prepackaged plans that allow for few substantive design decisions. In the case of a small business, for which budgets are limited, this makes sense. In the case of a larger business that has complex workforces or multiple locations, there is a general need to undergo a substantive design process.

A group of employee representatives, rather than a single employee should make these important front-end decisions, but the latter tends to be the common practice. It is difficult for someone close to the plan to predict how employees in any given case will perceive the plan and its various elements. It is also difficult for one person to have an accurate perspective on how employees will interpret a plan's provisions. For these reasons, it is useful to include employee representatives in the plan design process. This participatory process can not only help formulate the most appropriate design choices, but also can be used to position the plan with employees as something that they helped to create and implement.

In designing a 401(k) plan, the new plan sponsor will be faced with a number of decisions:

- What is the plan sponsor's corporate structure?
- Will the plan use individually drafted documents or prototype documents?
- What do the eligibility and vesting provisions in the plan involve?
- What types of contributions will the plan permit and require?
- What other plan options should be incorporated in the plan?

All of these are vital determinations because they will largely influence the plan's success or failure. These design decisions should be made with careful consideration and with a full understanding of the implications of the alternatives.

## PLAN SPONSOR

Frequently, more than one employer sponsors a single plan. The relationship of the employers to each other determines how the Code and ERISA will treat multiple employers sponsoring a single plan. There are three basic terms that describe plan sponsors, they are as follows:

- A single employer plan is a plan that is maintained by one employer or a group of related employers that form or are a part of a single controlled group (see Chapter 5 for a detail of controlled group)[8]
- A multiple employer plan generally is a plan that is maintained by two or more employers that are not members of a single controlled group and that is not a multiemployer plan[9]
- A multi-employer plan that is maintained under one or more collective bargaining agreements and to which more than one employer is required to contribute[10]

# PLAN DOCUMENTATION

One of the early decisions that the plan sponsor makes is whether to adopt a prototype plan or to have a plan custom-designed. A prototype plan is one that provides standardized language that is normally used in plans that are routinely approved by the IRS. Many major financial institutions that service this marketplace make available IRS-approved prototype plans. In addition, many attorneys that service this marketplace use prototype plans prepared by document service organizations.

In order to adopt such a plan, the sponsor executes an adoption agreement and selects various plan options. Some organizations offer what is called a flexible preapproved prototype document, which allows the plan sponsor to select various options in the design phase of the plan with the knowledge that the IRS has already approved the plan for use by the clients of the financial institution. In other words, the plan does not have to obtain separate IRS approval. In addition, provided the plan sponsor registers with the financial institution as an adopting employer, it is the responsibility of the financial institution that maintains the prototype document to keep the plan updated and current with any changes in pension law that might affect it.

This can represent a large savings in legal costs to plan sponsors because the registration fee is nominal. This is particularly true in there are of 401(k) plans where the plan options are relatively limited and standardized.

Although a flexible prototype document can represent some savings, it is only as good as the entity that uses it. In other words, even if the prototype document itself is very good, if it is being completed for the plan sponsor by a person with

---

8    Internal Revenue Code §414(b).
9    Internal Revenue Code §413(c).
10   Internal Revenue Code §414(f); ERISA §3(37).

no technical plan experience, there is no way to predict whether the plan will be successful. In short, the prototype document is a tool, and some are better than others are. No prototype plan document is good if the person who uses it lacks understanding of or perspective on qualified plan design.

Alternatively, many prospective plan sponsors desire to or have been told to adopt an individually designed 401(k) drafted by a pension attorney. The argument in favor of custom-designed plan documents is that they permit options that are more flexible and allow for easier amendment. Under the IRS's volume submitter program, a practitioner can gain blanket approval for the standard language used in all of its plan documents and request IRS approval only on the language of the plan that varies from the preapproved language.[11] This may be the best solution to the prototype-versus-custom plan for many sponsors, because it provides the convenience and cost savings of a prototype document, the ability to provide specific customized language provisions appropriate for their individual company requirements, and a competent advisor.

Thus, the real advantage that comes with a so-called custom document is the likelihood that the people drafting it will have knowledge of plan design and administration and will be less likely to provide inappropriate plan provisions in a given situation.

Whether the plan sponsor uses a prototype or customized document or something in between the most important element is the person or people who are advising the client with respect to the design features to be incorporated. Here, the level of experience and depth of knowledge of the individual organization involved is the most relevant inquiry.

## Determination Letter

If an employer decides not to use a preapproved prototype document, the sponsor has the option to seek advance determination about the qualified status of its retirement plan by the IRS. This written application procedure results in the issuance of a determination letter. A favorable response from the IRS indicates that in its opinion, the plan meets all the criteria needed for it to be deemed qualified under the Internal Revenue Code, if the plan complies, in operation, with applicable rules.[12]

Note that the receipt of a determination letter is not an absolute requirement under the Code or the IRS regulations. However, as a practical matter it makes inherent good sense to undergo this procedure because it will provide

---

11   Rev. Proc. 2000-20.
12   Internal Revenue Code §401(a).

the employer some assurance that its 401(k) plan is qualified under current law, and that it will remain so unless there are plan amendments or changes in the law (or if the plan does not comply in operation). Further, if the IRS examined the plan in the absence of a determination letter, the IRS may suspect that the plan is not in compliance and would subject it to intense scrutiny.

There are significant filing and procedural requirements associated with obtaining a determination letter. New plan sponsors are strongly encouraged to use professional counsel in this process.

## PLAN OPTIONS

The central part of the plan design process is the determination of what options and restrictions the plan will incorporate. Most of these decisions will have direct impact on the ability of the plan to satisfy the multitude of regulatory standards contained in the 401(k) regulations. These considerations fall within the following categories:

- Eligibility requirements
- Contribution types
- Vesting rules
- Investment provisions
- Distribution provisions

Each of these is discussed in turn here.

### Eligibility Requirements

As discussed at length in Chapter 4, specific minimum eligibility requirements apply to 401(k) plans. Generally, the plan cannot provide for eligibility criteria that require an employee to complete any more than one year of service or to be older than 21 years. Some plans have opted for a shorter, more permissive eligibility provision under the theory that it could be used as a recruiting tool. It has been pointed out, however, that as a practical matter, such an approach may be self-defeating, because it allows larger numbers of low-paid employees who generally do not participate in plans to become eligible, which in turn can cause the plan to fail certain discrimination tests. A plan cannot exclude employees for having attained a certain age.[13]

---

13    Internal Revenue Code §410(a)(2); ERISA §202(a)(2).

Although a plan may require one-year of service, in today's dynamic work environment allowing for immediate eligibility is the norm, with an entry as early as administratively feasible. Allowing entry at any time presents administrative problems, however. The alternative strategy of specifying multiple standard entry dates may make more sense and create a more manageable procedure, and generally enables eligible participants to join the plan on the next entry date following the date they become eligible.[14]

As will be noted in the discussion on vesting rules, there is an option to provide for a two-year eligibility period for employer nonelective (profit-sharing) contributions. However, if this option is used, the plan must provide for immediate vesting on these employer nonelective contributions. If the plan uses a waiting period of one year or less, the plan is permitted to establish a vesting schedule for both the matching and employer nonelective contributions.[15]

One of the biggest problems in administering eligibility requirements is in establishing data collection procedures to appropriately track employees' eligibility. This is particularly true in plans of larger employers that use decentralized payroll systems. As a result, the plan may either preclude eligible employees or include ineligible employees. The definition of eligibility is a fundamental determination in the operation of the plan, and the risk of not performing accurately this function is that the plan could be disqualified in the event of a plan audit. As a result, it is imperative for the plan administrator to assist the sponsor in designing a system to accurately calculate and administer eligibility standards.

## Contribution Types

Employer matching contributions are available and customary in many 401(k) plans. Of all plan provisions, employees are most vigilant to the availability of matching contributions. Although they are not required in 401(k) plans, the use of matching contributions can make or break the plan because they are a form of fringe benefit compensation. As Chapter 5 describes, the nondiscrimination rules restrict the unbridled use of matching 401(k) contributions and thus effectively require that lower-compensated employees participate in the plan at certain levels. The single most important factor influencing participation is the presence or absence of a company matching contribution.

Accordingly, it is essential for the plan sponsor and its advisors to seriously consider the type and level of the matching contribution that will be used. To

---

14  Internal Revenue Code §410(a)(1)(A)(i); ERISA §202(a)(1)(A)(i).
15  Internal Revenue Code §410(k)(2)(D).

do this, the sponsor first establishes a goal for participation that is based on employee demographics. This determination will help determine the level of match necessary in the plan. This determination is influenced by a number of factors:

- The type of organization and industry
- The average of the employee population
- The average number of years of service of the employees
- The marital status of the employee population

All of these factors influence the extent of the match necessary to make the plan successful and to meet the employer's participation goals. Ultimately, this determination needs to be made based on the judgment of an experienced plan consultant who can draw on similar experiences with similar clients. The employer can then operate under a calculated plan with some predicted probability of success.

If the sponsor normally makes a profit-sharing contribution, it should consider shifting some (or all) of this contribution into matching dollars. Generally, plan participants will see the matching contribution as a more concrete benefit than the more nebulous profit-sharing contribution.

During the design process, the plan sponsor should consider the structure of the matching contribution. A common matching contribution might provide a match of fifty percent of the first six percent of compensation contributed by the participant.

Nonelective employer contributions (in other words, profit-sharing contributions) are another possible source of contributions. There is usually a provision for such discretionary contributions because 401(k) plans are normally established as part of a profit-sharing plan.

Another source of contributions is employee after-tax contributions. The ability for an employee to make such contributions depends on the availability of such an option in the plan. Note that when such an option is offered in a plan, these contributions are subject to discrimination testing, as described in Chapter 5. Likewise, additional regulations[16] specify that a plan cannot condition a participant's ability to make after-tax contributions on his or her participation in the pretax plan. Because there are fewer restrictions on a participant's ability to access the after-tax contributions, participants sometimes make these contributions, participants sometimes make these contributions instead of pretax contributions when given the choice.

---

16    Internal Revenue Code §401(a)(27).

Finally, so-called top-heavy contributions must be made in a plan that is top-heavy in any given year. Briefly, a plan is top-heavy if the total amount of the accounts of the key employees exceeds 60 percent of the total accounts for all employees. In such a case, there is a minimum top-heavy contribution requirement imposed on the sponsoring organization. Because such contributions will represent a hard dollar cost to the sponsor, the possible requirement for such contributions should be considered in a new plan's design and planning phase. The conditions for top-heavy contributions are discussed in Chapter 5.

## Vesting and Forfeitures

One of the major features of the 401(k) plan is the optional requirement to provide for vesting of benefits according to a specific schedule set forth in the plan. As Chapter 4 describes, vesting represents the nonforfeitable interest of participants in their account balances. Vesting is only an issue with respect to the employer matching contributions and nonelective discretionary contributions. Employee elective deferrals are always 100 percent vested.

As discussed at greater length in Chapter 4, a plan may adopt two alternative vesting schedules to ensure compliance with IRS regulations. These include three-year "cliff" vesting and six-year "graded" vesting. Although a plan may provide for more liberal vesting, it may not require more restrictive standards than these two alternative systems.[17] The determination of which vesting schedule to use depends on a variety of factors, including the normal or average turnover of employees. The graded system of vesting clearly rewards longevity.

In addition, as discussed earlier, to the extent that a plan institutes anything greater than a one-year eligibility requirement for the allocation of employer contributions, the plan must provide for immediate vesting on such contributions.[18]

Finally, to the extent that nonelective employer (profit-sharing) contributions and matching contributions are used to satisfy the actual deferral percentage (ADP) test, they may not be subject to a vesting schedule. Rather, employees must be immediately 100 percent vested on such contributions.[19] This is discussed at length in Chapter 5.

If the plan is subject to a vesting schedule on matching and employer contributions, the decision must be made about what to do with the contributions that are forfeited by employees who leave the plan before becoming fully vested. There are three permissible uses[20] for plan forfeitures:

---

17  Internal Revenue Code §401.
18  Internal Revenue Code §410(a)(1)(B)(i).
19  Internal Revenue Code §411(a)(1).
20  ERISA §§403(c)(1) and 404(a)(1)(A).

- Reallocation to remaining participants
- Reduction of next employer contribution
- Restoration of accounts of returning participants who make repayments or reduction of administrative costs of the plan[21]

## Investment Provisions

The portion of the plan design process devoted to the selection and parameters of the plan investments is crucial for a number of reasons. First, from the standpoint of satisfying the fiduciary standards of the Employee Requirement Income Security Act (ERISA), this process must be undertaken with considerable prudence. Second, the actual investment performance of the investment vehicles will be closely scrutinized by employees and ultimately will influence the success or failure of the plan.

The first decision that the plan sponsors must make is whether to design the plan to provide for participant-directed investments or to maintain an employer-directed plan in which the plan fiduciaries make investment decisions for the entire plan. There are pros and cons to each approach; they are considered at length in Chapter 7 and Chapter 8.

Some plans allow participants to invest their money in virtually any investment vehicle. This can be problematic from an administrative standpoint, due to the difficulty of valuing, tracking, and reporting on an unlimited universe of possible investment options. It also creates potential problems under ERISA, insofar as the trustees must scrutinize the investments to be sure that none of them result in prohibited transactions or unrelated business taxable income.

Another design issue pertaining to the investment component of the plan is the frequency with which the plan will allow participants to make investment changes. Today's industry standard dictates that participants be given the ability to change investments as frequently as daily.

## Employer Stock Shares

If an employer decides to make employer stock an investment option under the plan, proper monitoring will include ensuring that those responsible for making investment decisions, whether the named fiduciary, investment manager, or participant, have critical information regarding the company's financial condition so that they can make informed decisions about the stock.

---

21  The use of forfeitures to pay for administrative expenses of the plan should be documented and the expenses should be legitimate and reasonable (See DOL Advisory Opinion 93-06A).

Many employers offer their own stock as investment options in their 401(k) plans or make their matching contributions in employer stock. If the stock of the company is publicly traded, there are no real restrictions on an employer's ability to offer its stock in the plan. However, it should be noted that offering company stock as an investment option does subject the plan to some SEC requirements.[22] Moreover, in those instances where employer stock is thinly traded, there are potential fiduciary concerns.

In addition, as a practical matter, employers should be sensitive to some of the issues that arise when employer stock is offered in the plan. First, to the extent that the stock fails to perform adequately, participants who have invested their 401(k) accounts in the employer stock will be extremely frustrated and disappointed. This is quite possible when the employer stock is thinly traded. In addition, from an administrative standpoint, employer stock that is not publicly traded creates some valuation issues, particularly if the plan is attempting to run on a frequent valuation system (unless the sponsor chooses to rely on prior independent appraisals). Employer stock is considered at greater length in Chapter 6.

## Participant Loans

Loan provisions in 401(k) plans are extremely popular.[23] A large percentage of all 401(k) plans offer their participants the ability to borrow money from the plan. In determining whether to offer plan loan provisions, prospective plan sponsors should be cognizant not only of the specific regulations relating to participant loans but also to the perception that the availability of loans will have on participants.

In promoting a new plan, one of the largest challenges to plan sponsors is convincing employees to defer a percentage of their income into the plan. One of the difficulties in this is convincing employees that it makes economic sense to participate even in light of the penalties for premature distributions. One way around this negative perception is to make loans available in the plan. In this manner, employees are more apt to participate in the plan knowing that in the event of an emergency they will be able to access a portion of their funds without tax liability.

However, loans are administratively and legally complex, and care should be taken to understand the parameters governing loans. More care should be taken in selecting a plan administrator with superior capabilities in the area of loan administration and record keeping. This will be discussed in Chapter 6.

---

22   17 C.F.R. §230.428(a)(1).
23   How Effective Is Inv. Advice in Influencing Asset Allocation? IOMA's Report on Managing 401(k) Plans, n o04-10 (Oct 2004).

## Dollar Limitations

To the extent the loan regulations are followed in designing and maintaining a participant loan program, the loans themselves will not be treated as taxable distributions. The major restriction on loans involves specific loan dollar limitations. In general, a loan must not exceed the following:[24]

1. The lesser of $50,000 minus the excess of the highest outstanding balance of loans from the plan during the one-year period ending on the day before the date on which such loan was made, over the outstanding balance of loans from the plan on the date such loan was made; or

2. The greater of one-half the present value of the employee's vested benefit under the plan or $10,000.

## Repayment Periods

In order to avoid being treated as a taxable distribution, a plan loan to a participant must be repaid within five years. If, however, the plan loan is used to purchase a principal residence for the employee, the repayment period can be extended. In actuality, there is no regulatory limit on the repayment period for principal residence loans, although 10 to 15 years is customary.

In addition to the required payment periods, the loan repayment schedule must provide for level amortizations. This term simply means that the loan repayments must be made in substantially equal installments of principal and interest. In addition, such repayments may not be made any less frequently than quarterly.

Most plans that provide for loans include a provision to accelerate the loan in the event of a participant's termination from employment, death, or disability.

## Prohibited Transaction Rules

As will be discussed in Chapter 7, certain transactions (including loans) are generally prohibited if they occur between a plan and a party-in-interest. The party-in-interest includes participants in the plan. Therefore, a loan between a plan and a participant might be deemed a prohibited transaction under ERISA and the Internal Revenue Code. Recognizing this, Congress authorized the IRS and DOL to issue exemptive criteria so that loans could be provided to participants under certain conditions.[25]

---

24    Internal Revenue Code §72(p)(2).
25    Internal Revenue Code §401(a)(13)(A).

The criteria for loans are as follows:

- They must be available to all participants and beneficiaries on a reasonably equivalent basis.
- They must not be made available to highly compensated employees in a discriminatory manner.
- They must be made in accordance with the provisions of the plan.
- They must bear a reasonable rate of interest.
- They must be adequately secured.

The DOL's regulations for participant loans provide for loans to be generally available and to not violate the directive that they are provided on a reasonably equivalent basis even if the plan provides a minimum loan requirement of $1,000. This is suggested for administrative convenience.

The rate of interest that should be charged is governed under the regulations as well, which provide that the rate should be commensurate with the prevailing interest rate charged by a business making similar types of loans. This is difficult to follow because no other businesses make loans to participants using their vested balances as collateral. Therefore, many plans use a formula such as the prime rate plus one or two percent.

Further, the regulations require the loan to be secured by the participants' vested balance or by outside collateral. However, no more than one-half of the participants' vested balance may be used to secure the loans. For this reason most plans tend to limit participants' loans to 50 percent of their vested balance even if the participants might technically be able to borrow more than the amount in order to avoid having outside collateral.

Finally, no portion of the participants' vested balance may be used as security for a loan unless the participants' spouse consents to the loan (if the plan is subject to the joint and survivor annuity requirements).

## Hardship Withdrawals

With the exception of participant loans, the only way that participants can access employee contributions is in the case of hardship. However, in order to receive a hardship withdrawal, the plan document must allow for such an action. Like the loan provision, a hardship provision enhances plan participation in the initial stages of enrollment because employees feel that they have the ability to access their money in the event of an emergency. Conversely, like the loan provision, the hardship provision imposes considerable administrative responsibilities on the sponsoring organization.

Under the regulations governing hardship withdrawals, it is the responsibility of the employer to determine whether the participant has demonstrated a true hardship.[26] This is a substantial responsibility in view of the fact that a failure to comply with these regulations can result in disqualification of the 401(k) plan. In making these determinations, plan sponsors can look to the regulations that set forth a two-pronged test for hardship:

- The participant must demonstrate that he or she has an immediate and heavy financial need
- The withdrawal is necessary to satisfy the need

In order to determine whether the requisite need is present, employers can apply the facts and circumstances test. This is a burdensome test for employers because it requires a representative of the employer to review the facts and circumstances in each individual case to determine whether they create an immediate and heavy financial need. Therefore, plans that use this test need to create their own rules for allowing hardship.

The second part of the test, as noted earlier, requires the employer to determine whether the withdrawal is necessary to satisfy the need. This test is satisfied if it can be concluded that the amount of the withdrawal does not exceed the amount needed to relieve the financial need and the need cannot be satisfied from other resources reasonably available to the participant. This determination is made based on relevant facts and circumstances.

Now, the employer can rely on a written representation by the participant that the withdrawal is necessary for the purposes stated earlier and that the need cannot be satisfied through any of the following:

- Reimbursement or compensation by insurance
- Liquidation of the employee's assets
- The employee's cessation of plan contributions
- Other distributions or nontaxable loans from any other plan in which the participant participates
- Borrowing from commercial sources at reasonable terms

---

26    Internal Revenue Code §401(k)(2)(B)(i)(IV).

## *The Safe Harbor Test*

As an alternative to the facts and circumstances test, plan sponsors can use the more restrictive safe harbor tests set forth in the IRS regulations.[27] The safe harbor regulations were established so that employers would have greater certainty about whether the hardship withdrawal requirements were satisfied in any given case. Under the safe harbor test[28], a hardship will be considered to be made for reasons of immediate and heavy financial need for any of the following reasons:

- Certain medical expenses for the participants, their spouses, or their dependents
- Purchase of the participant's principal residence (but not for mortgage payments)
- Payment of tuition and related educational expenses for the next twelve months for postsecondary education for the participants, their spouses, or their children or dependents
- Payments necessary to prevent eviction from a participant's principal residence or foreclosure on the mortgage of the participant's residence

If a plan adopts the safe harbor test as the standard for hardship withdrawals, only those conditions just mentioned will permit such a withdrawal, and other severe financial needs cannot justify a distribution.

The final determination that must be made under the safe harbor test is whether the withdrawal is necessary to satisfy the requisite immediate and heavy financial need. Under the test, the employer is permitted to rely on the participants' representation that the amount of the withdrawal does not exceed the amount necessary to satisfy the need and that all of the following requirements are satisfied:

- The participants have made all withdrawals and nontaxable loans available under all plans maintained by the employer
- The plan must limit participants' deferral into the plan for at least six months after receipt of the hardship distribution
- When participants resume contributing to the plan, the maximum contribution the participants can make in the first year is reduced by the amount of the elective contribution made in the year in which the hardship withdrawal was made

---

27   IRS Notice 98-52.
28   Treas. Reg. §1.401(k)-1(d)(2)(iii)(B).

# CHOOSING THE PLAN TRUSTEE

With limited exceptions, section 403 of ERISA requires all assets of an employee benefit plan to be held in a trust by one or more trustees. As a practical matter, this requires that a trust document be executed in conjunction with the establishment of the plan itself. The trustees need to be named in the trust document or plan document, or at least appointed by the named fiduciary in the plan. The named fiduciary refers to one or more representatives designated in the plan instrument by name or by title responsible for the plan operation. The named fiduciary requirement provides employees or other interested parties with the ability to ascertain the person responsible for plan operations.

There are two basic choices to be made in determining who shall act as trustee:

- Whether the employer should appoint one or more corporate officers or employees to act as trustee(s) over the plan
- Whether the plan should appoint a professional or institutional trustee (that is, a trust company)

As a practical matter, the presence of an institutional trustee is an effective way for plan fiduciaries to manage their responsibilities under ERISA. Although the plan fiduciaries may not absolve themselves of potential liability, the act of appointing an institutional trustee effectively transfers the fiduciary responsibility associated with trusteeship to the corporate trustee.

In addition, the presence of an institutional trustee can serve as a safety net to plan fiduciaries. The trustee's responsibilities are generally construed widely by courts and by the DOL. This can mean that a trustee has a responsibility beyond merely the assets deposited with it. Rather, a good trustee will act in a quasi-supervisory and enforcement role over the plan.

In addition, the inclusion of an institutional trustee for plan oversight can sometimes eliminate the need for a fiduciary bond, as required under section 412 of ERISA. The bonding regulations are complex and are beyond the scope of this book. However, to the extent that the company personnel never handle participants' funds (as defined precisely in the bonding regulations), the presence of an institutional trustee may obviate the need for bonding.

Finally, the presence of an institutional trustee goes a long way toward making participants comfortable about the plan. Participants usually feel better knowing that a recognizable institutional trustee that is regulated by banking laws and ERISA is holding their assets. Although the trust is impenetrable regardless of whether the assets are trusted by an individual or by an institution, there is clearly a different perception of the two by plan participants.

In the event that the plan appoints a corporate trustee, there will need to be express language in the trust agreement that sets forth the scope and limit of the trust relationship. In most instances, professional trustees maintain their own prototype trust agreements that specify the conditions of the trust relationship. Frequently, however, the plan sponsor may want to have its attorneys draft their own trust agreement to govern the trust. Most institutional trustees are comfortable with using custom-designed trust agreements, if certain language is included in the document and that it does not create responsibilities that the trustee cannot or will not be able to fulfill. One example of a commonly requested provision is an indemnification by the trustee for all fiduciary problems that might occur in the plan. Whereas such a provision is desirable from the employer's standpoint, it is impermissible as a matter of law for plan assets to be used to indemnify fiduciaries in their breaches.[29]

# PLAN ADMINISTRATION

The final element of concern in the establish and design phase of the plan is the administrative component of the plan. Plan administration deals with four primary responsibilities:

- Plan record keeping, discrimination testing, and government reporting
- Payroll reduction and tax compliance
- Distribution processing
- Implementation of participant investment directions

All of these items are considered at length in Chapter 5.

# QUALIFICATION FAILURES

In spite of diligent efforts to follow the applicable sections of the Code, ERISA, or applicable regulations, an employer still may make a mistake. To the extent that a plan has been operated in a manner that violates even the most technical provisions of the IRS 401(k) regulations, the plan may have subjected itself to disqualification for the period of time that it violated any such provision. This can result in substantial tax liability on the part of both employer and employees.

---

29   ERISA §410(b). However, a non-breaching fiduciary may be reimbursed by a plan for reasonable expenses, including legal fees incurred in his duties for the plan and undertaken for the exclusive behalf of the plan (See State St. Bank & Tr. Co. v. Salovaara, 326 F.3d 130 (2d Cir. 2003).

The IRS has established programs for employers that wish to correct plan defects that raise qualification issues. These programs are consolidated under the Employee Plans Compliance System (EPCRS). EPCRS consists or the following three programs[30]:

- **Self-Correction Program (SCP).** A plan sponsor that has established compliance practices and procedures may correct insignificant operational failures at any time without paying any fee or sanction. In addition, a plan that is the subject of a favorable determination letter may correct significant operational failures within a two-year period without paying any fee or sanction.

- **Voluntary Correction Program (VCP).** A plan sponsor, at any time before an audit, may pay a limited fee and receive the IRS's approval for the correction of a qualification failure. VCP includes special procedures for group and anonymous submissions.

- **Audit Closing Agreement Program (Audit CAP).** If a qualification failure is identified on audit, the plan sponsor may correct the failure and pay a sanction. The sanction imposed will bear reasonable relationship to the nature, extent, and severity of the failure, taking into account the extent to which correction occurred before audit.

---

30    Rev. Proc. 2003-44, 2003-25 I.R.B.

# Chapter 4—401(k) REGULATORY BASICS

As is the case with all qualified employee benefit plans, 401(k) plans are highly regulated under the Internal Revenue Code and ERISA. Nearly every aspect of the plan is subject to extensive regulations that are relatively complex and difficult to understand. To further complicate matters, these regulations undergo routine changes. As a result, few people except for practitioners actually feel comfortable dealing in the 401(k) regulatory environment.

The purpose of this chapter is not to deal with the 401(k) regulations with absolute precision. Rather, the purpose of this chapter is to deal with the main regulatory concepts in a way that nonpractitioners (specifically, plan fiduciaries, benefit managers, and their advisors) can appreciate and understand how these plans function and are regulated. For this reason, not all provide specific statutory and regulatory citations are provided because to do so would detract from the overview nature of this book. The following figure illustrates the range of possible contributions to a 401(k) plan:

## Figure 4-1: Contribution Types

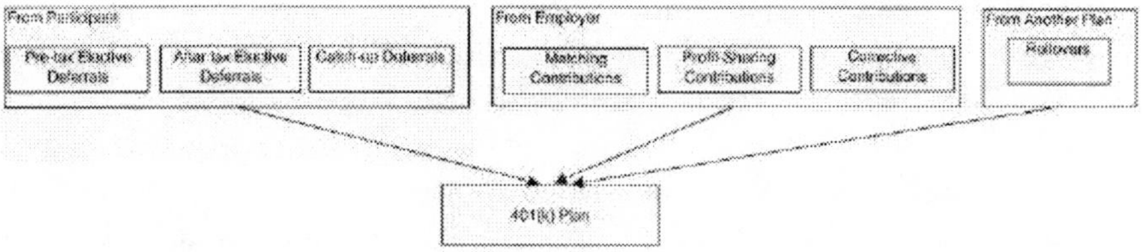

## CASH OR DEFERRED ARRANGEMENTS

A 401(k) plan is part of a qualified profit sharing or stock bonus plan that contains what is known as a cash or deferred arrangement (CODA). All 401(k) plans by definition permit CODAs. For this reason, the terms 401(k) and CODA are used interchangeably, though technically the CODA is merely a feature of the 401(k) plan. In actuality, the term 401(k) governs only the employee's elective contributions (that is, the CODA). Other types of contributions are governed under different sections of the Code. Yet, it is common for employers and employees to use 401(k) in reference to the whole plan.

The term CODA refers precisely to the ability of an eligible employee to elect to have his or her employer either contribute to the plan on the employee's behalf or pay an equivalent amount to the employee in the way of cash compensation. This election by the employee most commonly takes the form of a compensation reduction agreement in which the employee elects to reduce his or her cash compensation and have the employer contribute that compensation to the plan on the employee's behalf.

The amount contributed to the plan under the CODA is called an elective contribution, which is subject to certain limitations. For the most part, elective contributions are excluded from an employee's gross income in the year in which they are made and are, therefore, not taxed until distributed. One confusing aspect of elective contributions is that even though they are technically deferrals made by employees, many of the myriad 401(k) regulations issued by the IRS consider elective contributions to be made by the employer.[31]

Many 401(k) plans include other types of contributions, including after-tax contributions. Such contributions are known under the regulations as employee contributions and are made from an employee's after-tax earnings.[32] Another source of contributions includes those made by the employers that are tied in some way to the amount of employee elective contributions. These are called matching contributions.

The final type of contributions common in such plans is nonelective contributions. Such payments include other employer contributions such as discretionary profit-sharing contributions.

Elective contributions, matching contributions, and nonelective contributions made to a plan are not included in employees' gross income, provided that the plan follows the requirements for qualified status under the regulations. Income taxes are essentially postponed until the employee receives a distribution from the plan. Moreover, any earnings on the employee or matching contributions accumulate tax-free until the time of distribution.

# 401(k) PLAN BASICS

Special requirements apply to 401(k) plans in order for them to receive favorable tax treatment. These requirements, which are dealt with at length in the remainder of this chapter, are as follows:

---

31    See Internal Revenue Code §401(k)(4)(A).

32    Rev. Rul. 93-87.

- Eligibility: The 401(k) plan may not create conditions for eligibility that exceed one year of service
- Coverage requirements: As is the case with any qualified plan, minimum coverage and participation requirements must be satisfied
- Employee elections: The plan must permit eligible employees to elect to have the employer make a contribution on behalf of the employee or to receive the same amount in compensation
- Contribution limits: The amount of elective contributions made on behalf of each employee must not exceed specific limits
- Employee's rights: The plan must establish nonforfeitable rights to employee elective contributions
- Conditional benefits: With the exception of employer matching contributions, the plan may not condition the receipt of any other type of benefits on participation in the 401(k) plan through elective contributions
- Plan distributions: The plan must limit distributions to a number of specific instances
- Nondiscrimination: The plan must not discriminate in favor of any prohibited class of employees and must satisfy special nondiscrimination tests on an annual basis

## Minimum Eligibility Requirements

Generally, 401(k) plans are permitted to impose two eligibility requirements.[33] The first is known as the year of service requirement, which may require an employee to complete no more than one year of service before becoming eligible to participate in the plan. The second eligibility requirement that plans may impose is an age requirement. The maximum age requirement that a plan may impose for eligibility in the plan is twenty-one years.

## Years of Service

Most of the complexity and confusion regarding eligibility provisions revolves around the year of service calculation. A year of service is calculated generally as a twelve-month period beginning on the first day of employment during which an employee completes at least 1,000 hours of service. If the employee does not complete 1,000 hours of service during the initial eligibility computation

---

33    Internal Revenue Code §§ 410(a)(1)(B)(ii), 410(a)(1)(A)(ii).

period, the next period begins on the anniversary date of employment or, if provided in the plan, on the first day of the plan year during which the anniversary date falls.

In general terms, all years of service with the employer must be considered. This includes years of service with a predecessor employer if the successor employer maintains the predecessor's qualified plan. Service with any member of a controlled group or affiliated service group (that is, related employers) must be considered. Attention should be given to issues related to common law and leased or contracted employees, maternity or paternity leave, and military leave in determining years of service.

## Hours of Service

An hour of service is any hour for which an employee is paid or entitled to payment from an employer for his or her work. This includes periods of time during which no real work was performed where the employee nonetheless received compensation such as vacation, holidays, illness, jury duty, and other specified instances. Interestingly, an hour of service is defined under the DOL regulations to include any hour for which back pay is awarded.[34]

The DOL has the task of providing regulations to further develop the meaning of the term "hours of service."[35] These different approaches are permitted for administrative ease more than any other reason.

In any event, an employee who satisfies the minimum age and service requirements of a plan must be permitted to begin participating in the plan no later than the earlier of either of these dates:[36]

- The first day of the first plan year that begins after the employee has satisfied the eligibility requirements
- Six months after the date that the employee became eligible

As a practical matter, most plans can satisfy this requirement by allowing for quarterly entry dates into the plan.

---

34  DOL Reg. §2530.200b-3.
35  DOL Reg. §2530.200a-3.
36  Internal Revenue Code §§ 410(a)(1)(B)(ii), 410(a)(1)(A)(ii).

## Coverage Requirements

All 401(k) plans must satisfy one of the coverage tests in order to receive favorable tax treatment:

- Coverage of 70 percent of non–highly compensated employees
- The ratio percentage test
- The average benefit test

These tests are examined closely in Chapter 5.

## Employee Elective Contributions

### Pretax

Elective contributions are those contributions that are made to a plan by the employer on an employee's behalf pursuant to a CODA agreement. If the employee agrees to defer a portion of his or her compensation under the 401(k) plan, the amounts contributed to the plan are generally treated as employer contributions, even though technically the employee has directed the employer to contribute. Such contributions are not included in the employee's taxable income in the current year and are allowed to accumulate tax-free. If, however, the employee chose to receive the compensation directly in the form of cash, this compensation would be taxable. This in essence is a CODA.

Pretax elective contributions are made pursuant to a salary deferral agreement or compensation reduction agreement under which the employee directs the employer to reduce his or her current compensation by a specified amount and to contribute that amount to the plan on behalf of the employee.

To be valid, such agreements can be made only with respect to amounts that are not "currently available." In other words, the employee cannot have already received compensation or can readily receive it at his or her discretion. Rather, an amount is not currently available if the employee may not, under any circumstances, receive the compensation before a specified future date.[37]

### After tax

Some 401(k) plans permit employees to contribute on an after-tax basis. Unlike elective contributions, such contributions would not be excluded from any employees' taxable income. These contributions would, however, accumulate any earnings on a tax-free basis until they are withdrawn.

---

37    Treas. Reg. §1.401(k)-1(a)(3)(ii).

When such an option is available in the plan, the plan cannot condition the right to make such after-tax contributions on an employee's participation in the pretax CODA. In addition, the right to make such after-tax contributions may not discriminate in favor of "highly compensated employees", and certain tests are applied to ensure fairness to all employees, as discussed later.

## Catch-up

For those participants age 50 and older, the Code authorizes plans to permit elective pre tax contributions beyond the maximum deferral limits.[38]

## Rollover

Rollover contributions are participant assets from another qualified retirement plan. Although a plan is not required to accept rollover contributions, it may wish to do so to accommodate employees' desires to consolidate all of their employer-sponsored retirement funds.[39]

# Employer Contributions

Employees' elective deferrals are treated as employer contributions under the 401(k) regulations. The reason for this is that the employee has directed the employer to reduce his or her current compensation and to deposit the same amount directly into the plan. The employee, therefore, never receives the cash until he or she takes a distribution and is therefore not taxed until that time.

Employers are permitted to make other types of contributions for their employees. These have been noted earlier:

- Employer matching contributions
- Nonelective employer contributions
- Corrective contributions (see Chapter 5)

## Matching Contributions

A matching contribution is an optional contribution made by the employer that is allocated to employees purely based on employee or elective contributions. For example, in a plan in which the employer contributes fifty cents for every dollar of elective or employee contributions, the company is making a matching contribution.

To be qualified, matching contributions must satisfy certain requirements with respect to distribution, vesting, and nondiscrimination, as described later

---

38    Internal Revenue Code §414(v).
39    Internal Revenue Code §408(d)(3).

in the chapter. It is extremely important to be aware of these specific limitations, even without precisely knowing how they operate.

## Nonelective Contributions

A nonelective contribution is an employer contribution that is made to the plan (other than a matching contribution) that the employee could not have elected to receive in cash. Normally, such contributions are in the nature of traditional discretionary profit-sharing contributions.

As with matching contributions, to be qualified as nonelective, employer contributions are subject to certain specific requirements with respect to minimum coverage, distribution, vesting, and nondiscrimination.

## Contribution Limitations

Internal Revenue Code section 415 imposes a total limit on the combination of elective deferrals, employee after-tax contributions, nonelective employer contributions and employer matching contributions that may be contributed to a plan during any tax year for any particular employee. In general terms, for 2004, the combination of these contributions may not exceed the lesser of either $41,000 or 100 percent of the participant's compensation. Limitations imposed by Code section 401(a)(17), however for 2004 allow only the first $205,000, as adjusted by cost of living adjustments, in compensation to be used in order to calculate contribution limits.

In addition to the general section 415 limitations noted previously, there are also specific limitations under section 401(g) on the dollar amount that any employee may make in elective deferrals in any given tax year. Any employee deferrals in excess of this limit must be included in the taxable income of the employee for whom the deferrals were made and distributed.

The specific limitation on employee elective deferrals began in 1987 at $7,000, and has been indexed every year since with inflation as measured by the Consumer Price Index. In 2004, this limitation was $13,000.[40]

### Historical Deferral Limits

| | |
|------|----------|
| 2001 | $10,500 |
| 2002 | $11,000 |
| 2003 | $12,000 |
| 2004 | $13,000 |
| 2005 | $14,000 |
| 2006 | $15,000 |

40   Internal Revenue Code §402(g)(1).

After 2006, the Secretary of Treasury will adjust the limit, and any increase not a multiple of $500 shall be rounded to the next lowest multiple of $500.

Note that these limitations apply with respect to the employee's tax year, not the tax year of the plan. As a result, it is quite possible that an employee's deferrals could exceed these limitations in a calendar year if the plan year operates on a different schedule. It should also be noted that the limitation applies to the employee without regard to the number of plans in which he or she might participate. From the employer's perspective, however, it is the obligation of the employee to keep track of the total limit to the extent that he or she participates in different plans from different employers.

Additionally, employees who turn age fifty or older within the end of the plan year are permitted to make "catch-up" contributions that exceed the regular 401(k) contribution limits. That is, employees are allowed to contribute extra amounts over and above the before-tax contribution limit. Employers are not required to allow catch-up contributions. The before-tax contribution limit is increased as follows:

### *Yearly Catch-up Contribution Limit*

| | |
|---|---|
| 2002 | $1,000 |
| 2003 | $2,000 |
| 2004 | $3,000 |
| 2005 | $4,000 |
| 2006 | $5,000 |

## Top-Heavy Contributions

Recent changes to the top-heavy rules include a revised definition of "key employee" and the reduction of the five-year look back rule to one-year for distributions after the employee's separation from service.[41] Moreover, employer-matching contributions are taken into account in satisfying the minimum employer contribution requirement.

In addition to the normal qualification requirements, some plans are subject to additional requirements if they primarily benefit key employees. In the case of 401(k) plans, a plan is top-heavy if, as of the "determination date," the total of the accounts of all key employees exceeds 60 percent of the total of all employees. In those instances where a plan is deemed top-heavy, there is a minimum contribution requirement imposed upon the employer.

---

41   Internal Revenue Code §416.

Under a top-heavy 401(k) plan, the employer must contribute for each nonkey employee of at least three percent of compensation. However, if the highest contribution rate of a key employee is less than three percent, the three percent minimum contribution rate is reduced to that rate. In addition, a top-heavy plan is subject to different vesting requirements.

To determine whether a plan is top-heavy it is necessary to examine a number of intricate factors that are generally beyond the scope of this book. The plan administrator must examine such factors as the following:

1. Which employers must be treated as a single employer
2. What the determination date is for the plan year
3. Which employees are (or were) key employees
4. Which plans may be or are required to be aggregated for purposes of the test
5. The present value of the balances of key employees, former key employees, and nonkey employees

Although there are a great number of detailed regulations involved in the determination and application of top-heavy provisions, it is nonetheless useful to examine some of the basic regulatory provisions to understand how these regulations influences the operation of the plan.

Moreover, recent laws exempt a plan from top-heavy provision if the plan is a safe harbor plan, as described in Chapter 5.

## Determination of a Key Employee

The definition of key employee should not be confused with the definition of highly compensated employee for purposes of applying the nondiscrimination requirements, although there is clearly some overlap. A key employee is anyone who, during the plan determination year or any of the four preceding years, is (or was) any of the following:

1. An officer of the employer having an annual compensation of greater than $130,000 (as indexed)
2. A more than five percent owner of the employer
3. A more than one percent owner of the employer having an annual compensation from the employer of more than $150,000

Clearly, this technical definition defies simplification. Normally, the plan administrator will perform this top-heavy test as a matter of routine to determine whether the employer must make top-heavy contributions.

Once again, the top-heavy rules are extremely complex, and no attempt has been made to consider these rules at anything more than a superficial level. Those readers interested in learning more about these provisions are encouraged to refer to other sources.

In addition to the general contribution limitations, other complex rules prevent discrimination in favor of a class of employees called "highly compensated employees." These are discussed at length in Chapter 5.

## Vesting

As a practical matter, many 401(k) plans include a vesting schedule to encourage employees to remain employed by the sponsor. Generally, vesting schedules require an employee to remain employed by the sponsor and participate in the plan for a certain period in order to own 100 percent of the employer contributions. Any elective deferrals made by an employee to a plan are immediately 100 percent vested and nonforfeitable regardless of any vesting schedule. Vesting schedules apply only to employer contributions and matching contributions.

Although a plan may provide for more rapid vesting, Internal Revenue Code section 411 establishes minimum permissible vesting schedules. In reality, these are maximum permissible vesting schedules, because they establish limits on the amount of time that a plan may require an employee to vest in his or her benefits. In any event, the guidelines set forth the following[42] as permissible vesting structures:

- Three-year "cliff" schedule
- Six-year "graded" schedule

### Three-Year Cliff Vesting Schedule

Under the three-year cliff vesting approach, an employee is not vested in any amount until he or she has completed three years of service. Immediately after completing three years of service, the participant becomes 100 percent vested.

#### Example of Three-Year Cliff Vesting

| Years of Service | Percentage Earned |
|---|---|
| 1 | 0 |
| 2 | 0 |
| 3 | 100 |

---

42    Internal Revenue Code §§411(a)(2)(A), 411(a)(2)(B); Economic Growth and Tax Relief Reconciliation Act of 2001, Pub. L. No. 107-16, §633 (2001).

## *Six-Year Graded Vesting Schedule*

Under the six-year "graded" vesting approach, the employee accumulates his or her rights to employer contributions over a period of six years.

**Example of Six-Year Graded Vesting**

| Years of Service | Percentage Earned |
|------------------|-------------------|
| Less than 2      | 0                 |
| 2                | 20                |
| 3                | 40                |
| 4                | 60                |
| 5                | 80                |
| 6                | 100               |

Of course, these are only statutory minimums; a plan sponsor is always permitted to create a more liberal vesting schedule or to provide for immediate 100 percent vesting.

In applying these rules, a year of service is a precisely defined term. It is defined to include a calendar year, plan year, or any period consisting of twelve consecutive months during which the participant has completed 1,000 or more hours of service. The hour of service definition is the same one used for determining eligibility, discussed earlier.

## *Breaks In Service*

If there has been a break in service, an employee's service may be excluded for purposes of both vesting and eligibility. Under the vesting and eligibility rules, an employer is permitted to exclude prior years of service for any participant who is rehired after a one-year break in service until the employee has a new year of service. A one-year break in service is any calendar year, plan year, or other twelve-month consecutive period in which the participant has not completed at least 500 hours of service.

For example, assume that an employee had three years of service as of January 2002. At that time, the employee leaves employment for a period of one year, effectively taking a break in service. If that employee is rehired in January of 2003, at the time she is rehired her prior three years of service can be ignored for vesting purposes. However, if she completes one additional year of service, her prior years of service will be once again counted, and she will have four years of service for vesting purposes.

There are additional special rules dealing with breaks in service exceeding five consecutive years that should be consulted where applicable.

## Distributions

The 401(k) plan regulations provide fairly specific limitations with regard to distribution of plan assets. These limitations differ depending upon the type of contribution.

Pretax elective contributions may not be distributed before any of the following events:[43]

- Participant's separation from employment
- Participant's death
- Participant's disability
- Participant's reaching 59-and-a-half
- Participant's hardship
- Plan's termination

### Distributions for Reasons of Separation from Employment

If an employee separates from employment to the sponsor, elective contributions can be distributed without jeopardizing the qualified status of the plan. Separation from employment means that a participant has retired or has otherwise completely severed the employment relationship with the employer maintaining the plan. This new standard applies[44] to distributions on or after January 1, 2002, if a plan has been amended to adopt this new standard.

The new standard is not required, and employers may continue to use the old standard of separation of service. The most significant difference in the two standards is a concept known as the "Same Desk Rule."[45] Under the standard of separate from service, the employee must sever all employment relationships with the employer and its controlled group. The regulations defining controlled group can be consulted for further information. However, an acquired company's plan can make distributions to participants who continue to work for the buyer at the same job after the merger or acquisition.

### Distributions for Reasons of Disability

The Internal Revenue Code definition under section 72(m) is generally used but is restrictive. It defines disability as the inability "to engage in any substantial gainful activity by reason of any medically determinable physical or mental

---

43    Internal Revenue Code §401(k)(2)(B)(i).
44    IRS Notice 2001-57
45    Rev. Rul. 2000-27.

impairment which can be expected to result in death or to be of long contin-
ued and indefinite duration,"[46] Therefore, the Code provides that an individual will not be considered disabled unless he furnished proof of the disability
in the form or manner required by the IRS. There is no specific guidance as to
what form or in what manner proof must be furnished. Furthermore, IRS has
now taken the position that it will not issue a ruling as to whether a participant
will be considered disabled. A participant who is claiming to be disabled
should thus be prepared to support his claim by medical testimony or other
appropriate documentation which can be presented if his claim is challenged.

## Distributions for Reasons of Plan Termination

If a plan terminates, distributions of employee elective deferrals may be made
if the employer does not establish a successor plan or maintain another
defined contribution plan within the same controlled group. A successor plan
is defined to include any other defined contribution plan maintained or established by the same employer within twelve months of the distribution of all of
the assets from the plan.[47] If fewer than two percent of the eligible employees
of the terminated plan are eligible employees of the defined contribution plan,
it is not considered a successor plan.

## Tax Consequences of Plan Distributions

Although taxing distributions is generally an individual tax issue, it is
important to touch on the tax consequences of plan distributions. Amounts
distributed from the plan must be included in the gross income of the person who received the distribution. There are, however, limited exceptions
for distributions that qualify for lump-sum distribution or tax-free rollover
status. This is discussed later.

In the event that the distribution contains no employee after-tax contributions, the full amount of the distribution is taxable to the employee. If
employee after-tax contributions are included in the distribution, the amount
of after-tax contributions must be separated from the other contributions,
because tax has already been paid on that amount. Earnings on the after-tax
amount, however, are taxable.

Various regulations govern a person's ability to receive a lump-sum distribution
or a tax-free rollover into another qualified plan.

---

46   Internal Revenue Code §72(m).
47   Treas. Reg. §1.401(k)-1(d)(3).

### Form and Medium of Distributions

Broad discretion is granted when designing a 401(k) plan's distribution options. However, once a particular distribution form or medium is specified under a plan, the anti-cut back rules of Code section 411(d)(6) restrict the ability to amend or remove the form or medium of distributions.

### Tax-Free Rollovers

Another type of distribution that is afforded favorable tax treatment is a tax-free rollover into another qualified plan. Such rollovers may be made between plans to avoid 20 percent withholding tax and/or penalties. In order to be treated as a tax-free rollover, the distribution must be an eligible rollover distribution. Such distributions may be either total or partial distributions, each of which is precisely defined according to certain conditions.

There are particular requirements applicable to tax-free rollovers, and recipients of partial or total distributions should be advised to seek professional advice, particularly regarding the permissible rollover period (usually sixty days).

# DISCRIMINATION TESTING

In order to receive the special tax advantages of a qualified plan, the 401(k) plan must cover what is called a nondiscriminatory group of employees. In addition, the plan must have a minimum number of actual participants. Finally, there are express regulations that prohibit the contributions or benefits under the plan from discriminating in favor of "highly compensated employees."[48]

In general, in order for a plan to be qualified, it must satisfy the following requirements:

1. It must meet certain coverage requirements of the Internal Revenue Code.
2. All elective contributions must meet the nondiscrimination requirements of the IRS regulations.
3. All nonelective contributions must be nondiscriminatory.

---

48   Internal Revenue Code §410(b).

## Definitions and Concepts Used in Discrimination Testing

Throughout this and other chapters, specialized terms were used in the descriptions of the various required plan tests. All of these terms have precise meanings and are themselves subject to elaborate definitions and tests. As has been the common theme throughout this book, there is no attempt to define all of these terms and concepts with absolute precision because this would be beyond the scope of the book. Rather, here an attempt is made to deal with these terms and concepts on a fundamental level to give readers an understanding of the concepts used in regulating 401(k) plans.

Highly Compensated Employees (HCEs) is a term used throughout the 401(k) nondiscrimination regulations. The term itself is precisely defined under Internal Revenue Code section 414(g) and related IRS regulations. In essence, highly compensated employees are divided into two groups—active HCEs and former HCEs.

Generally, an active HCE includes any employee who during the current year and preceding year fulfilled any of the following criteria:[49]

1. An officer

2. A shareholder owning (directly or through related individuals such as spouses and lineal ascendants of descendants) more than five percent of the voting power or value of the employer

3. Any person who during the preceding year was an employee who received compensation of at least $90,000

4. A spouse or dependent of any of the foregoing

Each of these alternative definitions of HCEs is the subject of extensive regulations. The determination of who is an HCE in any given year is the responsibility of the plan administrator working with the employer. For purposes of this chapter, it is useful to understand that HCEs are the class of employees in favor of whom the plan may not discriminate.

Non–Highly Compensated Employees (NHCEs) include any employees who are not highly compensated under the previous definition.

---

49    Internal Revenue Code §414(q).

# Chapter 5—NONDISCRIMINATION AND TESTING CONCEPTS

In many respects, the nondiscrimination requirements applied to 401(k) plans are the essence of the 401(k) regulations. These nondiscrimination requirements appear in a number of forms throughout the regulations and seem to be the common thread throughout the varied and complex testing requirements. In essence, these requirements prevent the senior managers of an organization from providing themselves with a plan that is too heavily tilted in their favor. To prevent such bias, the 401(k) regulations reach a degree of technicality unmatched by other pension regulations.

The nondiscrimination requirements are so technically oriented that an entire book could be written devoted exclusively to describing the application of these rules. The intention in this book is merely to scratch the surface of these regulations so that the reader understands and appreciates the principles governing the nondiscrimination requirements under the 401(k) regulations.

There are actually three components to nondiscrimination under the 401(k) regulatory outline. First, the plan must satisfy the nondiscrimination coverage requirements under Internal Revenue Code section 410(b). Second, the plan must satisfy the minimum participation requirements under section 401(a)(26). Third, the plan must satisfy the nondiscriminatory contribution requirements pursuant to section 401(a)(4).

## MINIMUM COVERAGE RULES

Occasionally, for any number of reasons, an employer will not or cannot provide an identical benefit program to every employee of every related or affiliate company. However, in order for a qualified retirement plan such as a 401(k) plan to receive favorable tax treatment, the plan must cover a group of employees that is not discriminatory under section 410(b). A number of technical tests apply to make this determination. In essence, an employer is given some leeway in constructing a benefit program that does not cover every possible employee. As an alternative, an employer may exclude or treat differently certain types of employees and certain branches or locations if the resulting plan can satisfy the specific section 410(b) requirements.

A plan will be considered nondiscriminatory concerning coverage if it can pass one of the following tests:[50]

1. The plan must benefit at least 70 percent of the employer's non–highly compensated employees (the 70 percent test)

2. The plan must benefit a percentage of non–highly compensated employees that is equal to 70 percent of the percentage of highly compensated employees that benefit (the ratio-percentage test)

3. The average benefit provided test, which compares the average benefit of non–highly compensated employees with the average benefit of highly compensated employees

The 70 percent test is generally ignored because a plan that satisfies the 70 percent test will always satisfy the ratio-percentage test.

Before examining these tests, be aware that both the coverage and participation requirements permit the employer to exclude or treat separately certain groups of employees. Generally, employees who may be excluded include those covered under a collective bargaining agreement for which retirement benefits were the subject of bargaining, employees who do not meet the minimum eligibility requirements of age and length of service, employees of separate lines of business, nonresident aliens, and terminated employees. These excluded employees are not taken into consideration when a plan administrator performs the minimum coverage and participation tests. In addition, it should be recognized that a plan that includes no highly compensated employees (HCEs), as described in Chapter 4, does not have to satisfy any of the coverage tests.

In conducting these tests, the central inquiry is what number of employees is benefiting under the plan. To benefit under the plan, an employee generally needs only to be eligible to make elective contributions, whether or not he or she actually does so, and if the employee receives an allocation of employer contributions or forfeitures.

## The Ratio-Percentage Test

The ratio-percentage test assesses whether the number of non–highly compensated employees (NHCEs) who benefit under the plan equals at least 70 percent of the percentage of highly compensated employees who benefit under the plan. Although this test sounds simple, it is actually complex to administer and

---

50   Internal Revenue Code §410(b).

requires that the plan administrator consider a variety of factors. Numerous conditions apply in determining which employees to count in this test and which to exclude. For instance, in more complex corporate structures where there are related companies and/or parent-subsidiary relationships, the test requires that all the controlled group of employers be taken into consideration. The determination of who is included in the controlled group of employers is itself governed by some very complex regulations, as discussed later.

## The Average Benefit Test

As an alternative to the percentage ration test, the plan may satisfy the average benefit test pursuant to Internal Revenue Code section 410(b). This test assesses whether the plan benefits employees under a classification set up by the employer and found by the IRS not to be discriminatory in favor of HCEs and the average benefit percentage for the non–highly compensated employees equals at least 70 percent of the average benefit percentage of the HCEs. Thus, there are actually two parts under the average benefit test.[51]

### Part 1: Reasonable Classification

As noted, the classification that is set up by the employer to provide benefits must be reasonable and established under objective business criteria. Typically, such reasonable classifications include types of compensation (for example, salaried versus hourly employees), specific job categories, geographic locations, and other similarly benign classifications.

In addition, the classification so used must be found to be nondiscriminatory based either on a safe harbor rule or under a facts and circumstances test. Under the facts and circumstances test, the employer must demonstrate, among other things, the underlying business reason for the classification. The safe harbor rule is complex; it examines the percentage of non–highly compensated employees in conjunction with so-called safe and unsafe harbor percentages.[52] The complexity of this rule precludes us from examining it within the scope of this book.

### Part 2: The Average Benefit Percentage

In addition to the classification test, the plan generally must demonstrate that the benefits provided to non–highly compensated employees under all plans of the employer are equal to or greater than 70 percent of the benefits provided to

---

51    Treas. Reg. §1.410(b)-2(b)(2).

52    Id.

highly compensated employees.[53] As with the actual deferral percentage (ADP) test, the average benefit percentage test requires that the plan administrator determine an employee benefit percentage for each employee and then separately average these percentages for all employees. As with the other minimum coverage tests, this test is extremely complex and not easily summarized in lay terms. As is the case with all the discrimination tests, plan sponsors are strongly encouraged to retain a qualified plan administrator to manage test calculations.

# MINIMUM PARTICIPATION RULES

Apart from the coverage requirements applicable to qualified plans, every plan on its own must satisfy an additional minimum participation requirement under section 401(a)(26), whose purpose is to ensure that an employer does not create a benefit program for the sole purpose of providing benefits to an exclusive group of employees.

In general terms, the minimum participation requirements are satisfied only if the plan benefits the lesser of (1) fifty employees, or (2) 40 percent of all employees. It is important to understand that in contrast to the coverage requirements, aggregating different plans offered by the employer may not satisfy this requirement. Rather, each plan must satisfy this test on its own. This requirement effectively prevents employers from maintaining separate plans for highly and non–highly compensated employees.

# CONTROLLED GROUP RULES

In determining whether a plan satisfies the minimum coverage and participation requirements in more complex corporate structures, all employees of companies that are part of a "controlled group of employers"[54] are treated as if a single employer employed them. The purpose of this requirement is to prevent employers from separating highly and non–highly compensated employees by entity in an effort only to satisfy the nondiscrimination tests.

The relationship needed to be deemed part of a controlled group exists if an employer is a member of any of the following:[55]

---

53  Id.
54  Internal Revenue Code §§414(b), 1563.
55  Internal Revenue Code §§414(b), 1563, 414(m)(2), 414(c).

- A controlled group of employers
- A group of businesses under common control
- An affiliated service group

Under the first test, a controlled group of employers exists when there is either of the following:[56]

- A parent-subsidiary group consisting of a chain of corporations connected through at least 80 percent ownership of a controlling interest
- A so-called brother-sister group that consist of two or more corporations, each of which is at least 80 percent owned by five or fewer people, and these people together own more than 50 percent of each corporation

Of course, the determination of a controlled group requires the application of a complex definition to what may be complex facts. The other categories of controlled groups, groups of businesses under common control and affiliated service groups, are similarly complex.

## THE SEPARATE LINE-OF-BUSINESS RULES

Under the 401(k) regulations, there is an exception to the requirement that all controlled businesses be treated as one for purposes of the minimum coverage and participation requirements. Under the separate line-of-business exception, if an employer operates two or more separate lines of business, the coverage tests may be applied separately to each separate line of business.[57] The purpose of this exception is that it enables employers to provide different benefits packages to different business units without inadvertently violating the nondiscrimination requirements.

To be treated as a separate line of business, the employer must satisfy the IRS regulations defining separate lines of business. These regulations were issued under IRS Code section 414(r) for plan years beginning on or after January 1, 1993. The regulations governing separate lines of business are among the most complex parts of the 401(k) regulations. Plan sponsors seeking to use this exception should retain the assistance of qualified advisors.

---

56    Internal Revenue Code §§414(b), 1563.
57    Internal Revenue Code §414(r).

# NONDISCRIMINATORY CONTRIBUTION RULES

In addition to the tests just described, a 401(k) plan also must be nondiscriminatory insofar as it provides employees the ability to make elective contributions or to receive employer-matching contributions. Thus, the 401(k) regulations set forth a complex array of testing procedures designed to ensure that the rates of elective, matching, and after-tax contributions do no discriminate in favor of highly compensated employees. There are two separate but identical tests used to ascertain whether the contributions made by employees and employer are within permissible ranges under section 401(a)(4). These tests include the actual deferral percentage (ADP) test, described earlier, and the actual contribution percentage (ACP) test. The ADP test determines whether the amount of employee elective contributions satisfies the section 401(a)(4) nondiscrimination requirements. The ACP test determines whether the combination of employee after-tax and employer-matching contributions complies with the same nondiscriminatory requirements. Additionally, any employer matching contributions on Catch-Up Contributions are subject to nondiscrimination rules.[58]

Although the ADP and ACP test are separate inquiries and examine different sources of contributions, the formula used to apply each of the tests is identical. For simplicity's sake, we have dealt with these tests separately. However, observe that the ADP and ACP tests are elaborate and complex, and in may ways form the foundation of 401(k) plan regulation. As a result, the intention in this book is only to provide a foundation for understanding the general principles set forth by these tests, not to examine their precise application.

## The Actual Deferral Percentage Test for Elective Deferral

The ADP test is perhaps the central test applied to 401(k) plans and is the one most people think of if they know anything about 401(k) discrimination testing. It is designed to limit the extent to which elective contributions made on behalf of highly compensated employees exceed the contributions made on behalf of non–highly compensated employees. If the ADP test is satisfied, the plan is treated as satisfying the section 401(a)(4) requirements with respect to elective contributions only.

In essence, the ADP test tries to determine whether highly compensated employees are taking a significantly greater advantage of the plan than are the rank-and-file employees. The ADP test limits the unbridled use of 401(k)

---

58  Treas. Reg. §1.414(v)-1(b)(1)(iii).

arrangements by highly compensated employees by limiting their deferrals based on the deferrals of the other employees. If the plan fails its ADP test, corrective measures will have to be taken. Such corrective measures are discussed later.

The ADP test must be run each plan year to ascertain whether the plan complies with the strict nondiscrimination limitations. Several steps must be understood and followed to apply this test accurately. Note that these general steps are merely an overview and are not a substitute for the detailed application of these tests by a qualified professional plan administrator.

## Basic Mechanisms of the ADP Test

The ADP test asks the plan administrator to compare the actual deferral percentage of highly and non–highly compensated employees. This requires the calculation of the actual deferral ratio (ADR) for each employee. The ADR is merely the ratio of the employee's elective contribution to his or her compensation.

For example, if employee A, Joe Smith, earns compensation of $40,000 and makes elective deferrals of $2,000, his ADR is 5 percent. If employee B, Sara Johnson, earns compensation of $30,000 and makes no elective deferrals, her ADR is zero.

In making this determination, note that plans are permitted in some instances to treat nonelective and matching contributions as though they were elective contributions, provided certain requirements are met. For purposes of this discussion, note that this treatment has the effect of increasing the ADRs of eligible employees even if they did not contribute. This is because the plan can count what are essentially employer contributions as though the employees for purposes of calculating the ADR made them.

### Compute the ADP for both Highly and Non–Highly Compensated Employees

The next step in the ADP test process is to compute the ADP for both highly and non–highly compensated employees. The ADP for highly compensated employees is determined by taking the average of the ADRs for all highly compensated employees who are eligible under the plan. The same procedure is performed for all non–highly compensated employees eligible under the plan.

For example, consider Sample Company. Sample has six NHCEs who meet the plan's eligibility requirements. The employees make the following elective deferrals in their 401(k) plan:

|   | Compensation | Elective Contribution | ADR |
|---|---|---|---|
| A | $ 40,000 | $ 2,000 | 5% |
| B | $ 30,000 | $  0 | 0% |
| C | $ 25,000 | $ 2,500 | 10% |
| D | $ 30,000 | $ 2,500 | 8% |
| E | $ 42,000 | $ 2,940 | 7% |
| F | $ 35,000 | $  0 | 0% |
|   | Total ADR |  | 30% |
| **Highly Compensated** |  |  |  |
| G | $ 175,000 | $ 8,728 | 5% |
| H | $ 80,000 | $ 8,000 | 10% |
|   | Total ADR |  | 15% |

In the case of Sample Company, the ADP for the NHCEs is 5 percent (30 percent/6), and the ADP for the highly compensated employees) HCEs) is 7.5 percent (15 percent/2). As will be discussed later, this plan would fail the ADP test because the ADP for the HCEs exceeds the ADP of the NHCEs by more than the allowable margin.

## Compare the ADPs for both Highly and Non–Highly Compensated Employees

Once the plan administrator has performed the calculations just described to determine the ADPs for both highly and non–highly compensated employees, more than the allowable margin performs the actual ADP test to determine whether the ADP for the HCEs exceeds the ADP for the NHCEs. Generally, a plan will pass the ADP test if either of the following is true:

- The ADP for the HCEs does not exceed the ADP for NHCEs by more than a multiple of 1.25

- The ADP for the HCEs does not exceed the ADP for NHCEs by more than a multiple of two, if the ADP for the highly compensated employees does not exceed the ADP for the non–highly compensated employees by more than two percentage points. This is commonly knows as the 2.0/2 percent limitation

In the Sample Company example, the plan fails the ADP test in this particular plan year because of the following two facts:

- The ADP of the HCEs (7.5 percent) exceeds the ADP of NCHEs multiplied by a factor of 1.25 (5 percent × 1.25 = 6.25 percent)

- The ADP for the HCEs (7.5 percent) exceeds the ADP for the NHCEs (5 percent) by more than 2 percent

The following simple rule of thumb is useful in understanding the ADP test alternatives:

| ADP for NHCEs | Allowable ADP for HCEs |
| --- | --- |
| Less than 2 percent | Up to 2 times higher |
| Between 2 percent and 8 percent | Up to 2 percent higher |
| More than 8 percent | Up to 1.25 times higher |

Applying this simple rule of thumb to the Sample Company reveals that the highest contribution the HCEs would be permitted would be seven percent. Because the NHCEs are contributing at a rate of five percent, the application of the above rule would allow the NCEs to contribute at a rate two-percentage points higher.

### Excess Contributions Must Be Leveled and Corrected, if the Plan Has Failed the Test

An excess contribution is the excess of the elective contribution made by highly compensated employees over the maximum amount of contributions permitted under the plan's ADP test. For the Sample Company, the HCEs contributed at a rate of 7.5 percent, although the ADP test shows that there permissible ADP is only seven percent. The difference between these two numbers represents the excess contributions in the plan.

The application of the discrimination rules requires that these excess contributions be corrected within the twelve-month period following the year in which the plan failed its ADP test; otherwise, the plan will be disqualified for that year. These corrections must be made on an individual employee basis.

### *Leveling Excess Contributions*

The IRS regulations permit three methods to correct the excess contributions and cause the plan to retain its qualified status. Before the procedure for correcting excess contributions can be explained, it is necessary to understand the concept of leveling, which is the systematic reduction of individual HCE contributions until the excess contributions are eliminated. Leveling is nothing more than the process used to determine the amounts that must be corrected. Under the leveling principle, the actual deferral ratio (ADR) of the highly compensated employee with the highest ADR is reduced to the level needed to eliminate the excess contribution problem in the plan. If this not possible by reducing only one employee's ADR, then his or her ADR is reduced to the level of the next highest ADR. This process is repeated until the total plan excess contributions are eliminated and the plan passes its ADP test.

A simple example draws on the facts used in leveling. In the case of the Sample Company, the permissible ADP in the plan year is seven percent. Recall that the two HCEs were contributing 5 percent and 10 percent to the plan, respectively. Applying the leveling method, H's ADR would be reduced first to the level of the next highest ADR, even though G's compensation far exceeds that of H's. Thus, H's ADR is reduced to the extent necessary to correct the excess. This would require that H's ADR be reduced by one percent to a total ADR of nine percent.

After such an adjustment, the ADP for both HCEs would equal seven percent ((9 percent + 5 percent)/2), and the plan would satisfy the ADP test.

The process of leveling also requires that specific dollar amounts of excess contributions be determined by subtracting what the HCE with excess contributions was permitted to contribute under the plan form what he or she actually contributed. For the Sample Company, the amount of excess contributions made on behalf of H is $800 ($8,000—$7,200).

Note that this is an extremely simplified example of leveling. Depending on the size of the plan, leveling may require a systematic reduction of the contributions by multiple HCEs.

## Correcting Excess Contributions

After the leveling process, a plan must correct excess contributions in a timely manner to avoid penalties and possible disqualification of the plan. If the plan fails to correct excess contributions within two-and-a-half months following the end of the plan year in which they were made, the employer is subject to a 10 percent IRS penalty tax on the amount of excess contributions. If the excess contributions are not corrected before the end of the plan year following the year in which they were made, the plan will lose its qualified status for the plan year in which the excess contributions were made to the plan, as well as for all subsequent years until the excess contributions are corrected.[59]

Thus, it is extremely important to correct excess contributions in a timely manner. There are three ways to correct excess contributions in a plan that has failed its ADP test in a given year:[60]

- The excess contributions may be distributed to the appropriate HCEs as determined by the leveling method

- The HCE with excess contributions can elect to treat the overage as an elective after-tax contribution through a process called "recharacterization"

---

59    Internal Revenue Code §4979.
60    Treas. Reg. §1.401(k)-1(g)(10); Internal Revenue Code §401(k)(3)(A).

- The plan may make additional contributions for the NHCEs called qualified matching contributions (QMACs) or qualified nonelective contributions (QNECs)

Note that a plan is not limited to any one of these methods of correction but may employ combinations of them as long as the result is the required reduction of excess contributions.

## Distributing Excess Contributions

Perhaps the most commonly used method for correcting excess contributions is the distribution of excess contributions. Under this method, the excess contribution is distributed to the employee along with earnings (if any) on the excess contributions, and the total is treated as taxable income. Thus, in order to correct the excess contributions in this simple example, one option is for H to receive a taxable distribution of $800. In order to use this method of correction, the distribution must be characterized as a distribution of excess contributions, and it must be made within 12 months following the year in which the excess contribution was made. The plan administrator makes this decision.

If the excess contribution is made within two-and-a-half months following the end of the year in which the excess contribution was made, it is generally considered taxable income in the year in which excess contributions were made. If the distribution is made after that period, it is generally included in the employee's taxable income in the year in which it is received.

Note that the distribution of excess contributions is not generally subject to the normal restrictions and/or penalties applicable to plan distribution.

## Recharacterizing Excess Contributions

As an alternative to making a distribution, IRS regulations permit excess contributions to be converted to employee (after-tax) contributions and thus to remain in the plan using the method of recharacterization under the IRS regulations.[61]

Although the requirements and application of the recharacterization rules are rather complex, the principle itself is not. In essence, recharacterization permits excess contributions to remain in the plan and to continue to earn income in tax-free contributions to the plan. However, in order for the excess contributions to be converted, the employee will be required to pay income taxes on the recharacterized amount in the same way he or she would if that employee had received a taxable distribution of excess contributions. Through

---

61    Treas. Reg. §1.414(v)-1(d)(2)(iii).

this procedure, the employee has effectively converted (recharacterized) the contribution from a pretax to an after-tax contribution.

To be able to recharacterize excess contributions, the plan itself must have been drafted to accept employee after-tax contributions as of the first day of the year in which excess contributions were made. Otherwise, taxable distribution is the only method of correction. Furthermore, as will be discussed later under the actual contribution percentage test, the plan would be discriminatory if it limited employee after-tax contributions to recharacterized contributions.

Once again, note that the recharacterization rules are extremely complex and have significant impact on other testing requirements and limitations under the 401(k) regulations. An attempt has been made here simply to explain recharacterization as a concept and method to correct excess contributions. The application of this procedure demands the use of a qualified professional.

## Additional Contributions to Correct Excess Contributions

Once two-and-a-half months have elapsed after the end of the plan year in which excess contributions were made, additional contributions are the exclusive means of avoiding the 10 percent penalty tax on an employee's excess contributions. These contributions may be in the form of either qualified matching contributions (QMACs) or qualified nonelective contributions (QNECs).

Generally, matching contributions are tested separately under the ACP test. However, for purposes of passing the ADP test, the regulations permit the sponsor to treat any portion of QMACs as elective contributions. The practical result of this is that it permits the plan to count additional contributions that were made by the employer as employee elective deferrals and thus effectively increase the actual deferral percentage of NHCEs. The use of QMACs is extremely complex and involves a multitude of requirements and implications. As such, QMACs are not easily summarized in a primer such as this. Plan sponsors are strongly encouraged to seek the help of qualified plan administrators to determine whether the use of QMACs in the plan is practical.

In addition to QMACs, the nonelective QNECs can be treated as elective contributions for purposes of satisfying the ADP test. Once again, the effect is to treat employer contributions as employee elective deferrals in order to increase the actual deferral percentage among non–highly compensated employees. As with QMACs, the conditions for QNECs are extremely complex and raise issues well beyond the scope of this book.

## The Actual Contribution Percentage Test for Matching and After-Tax Contributions

In addition to the ADP test, a special nondiscrimination test required under Internal Revenue Code section 401(m), the actual contribution percentage (ACP) test, applies to employer matching contributions and to employee (after-tax) contributions under all defined contribution plans. Fortunately, the ACP test is identical to the ADP test for employee elective contributions except that it uses employer matching contributions and employee after-tax contributions as its testing base. As with the ADP test, the purpose of the ACP test is to ascertain whether the plan is discriminating in favor of HCEs.

### Basic Mechanisms of the ACP Test

The ACP is calculated by first determining the actual contribution ratio (ACR) for each eligible employee of the plan. This ratio is determined by dividing the sum of the employee's after-tax contributions and the employer's matching contributions by the employee's compensation. Referring back to the simple example, assume that the plan provides a 50 percent matching contribution and that it allows for employee after-tax contributions. Assume further the following facts:

| | Compensation | After-tax Contribution | Matching Contribution | ACR |
|---|---|---|---|---|
| Non–Highly Compensated | | | | |
| A | $ 40,000 | $ 0 | $ 500 | 1.25% |
| B | $ 30,000 | $ 0 | $ 0 | 0% |
| C | $ 25,000 | $ 0 | $ 625 | 2.50% |
| D | $ 30,000 | $ 0 | $ 225 | 0.75% |
| E | $ 42,000 | $ 0 | $ 630 | 1.50% |
| F | $ 35,000 | $ 700 | $ 350 | 3.00% |
| | Total ACR | | | 9.00% |
| | | | | |
| Highly Compensated | | | | |
| G | $ 175,000 | $ 3,950 | $ 2,182 | 3.50% |
| H | $ 80,000 | $ 0 | $ 2,000 | 2.50% |
| | Total ACR | | | 6.00% |

Thus, in the revised Sample Company example, the ACR for the NHCEs is 1.5 percent (9 percent/6 employees), and the ACR for the HCEs is 3 percent (6 percent/2 employees).

## Compare the ACR for both Highly and Non–Highly Compensated Employees

As with the ADP test, the ACP test requires a comparison of the ACPs of the HCEs and NHCEs to determine whether the ACP for the highly compensated employees exceeds the ACP for the non–highly compensated employees by a permissible margin. The same rule of thumb applies here as with the ADP test.

| ACP for NHCEs | Allowable ACP for HCEs |
| --- | --- |
| Less than 2 percent | Up to 2 times higher |
| Between 2 percent and 8 percent | Up to 2 percent higher |
| More than 8 percent | Up to 1.25 times higher |

Applying this rule of thumb to this simple fact pattern, the plan satisfies the ACP test, because the ACP for HCEs (3 percent) does not exceed twice the ACP for NHCEs (1.5 percent × 2 = 3 percent).

As noted earlier, a plan is required to apply the ACP test with respect to both matching contributions and employee after-tax contributions. However, if QMACs are treated as employee elective contributions for purposes of satisfying the ADP test, they do not have to satisfy the ACP test as well and may not be used to help employee after-tax contributions and other non-QMAC matching contributions satisfy the ACP test. It is important to note here that only those matching contributions used to satisfy the ADP test are excluded from the ACP test.

If the plan cannot satisfy the ACP test with respect to the matching and employee after-tax contributions, the plan is permitted to consider QNECs as employer matching contributions. As noted earlier for the ADP test, the use of QNECs is extremely complex and is beyond the scope of this book. As a practical matter, plan sponsors are advised to seek the guidance of a professional administrator in determining the use of QNECs.

## Determining Excess Aggregate Contributions and Make Necessary Corrections

Recall from earlier discussions that the effect of a failed ADP test is excess contributions. The same is true for a failed ACP test, for which the result will be excess aggregate contributions. These are the excess of the aggregate of employee after-tax contributions and employer-matching contributions made on behalf of highly compensated employees over the maximum amount permitted under the ACP test.

As is the case with excess contributions under the ADP test, excess aggregate contributions under the ACP test must be corrected on an individual employee basis. This requires the application of the identical leveling process described in the discussion of the ADP test.

There are two ways to correct excess ACP amounts:

1. The plan can distribute excess aggregate contributions to the HCEs or forfeit nonvested excess aggregate contributions.

2. The employer can make additional matching contributions.

### Distributing Excess Aggregate Contributions

The primary method of correcting a highly compensated employee's share of excess aggregate contributions is for the plan to make a distribution of the share plus any income to the employee. However, if any of the excess aggregate contributions are not vested under the plan, they may be forfeited rather than distributed. Note that vested matching contributions may not be forfeited by HCEs for purposes of correcting excess aggregate contributions.

Although the distribution-or-forfeiture rules applicable to excess aggregate contributions are generally complex, there are several principles that are appropriately discussed within the scope of this book. Ordinarily, the employer will distribute first any matching contributions that were made in connection with elective contributions that were required to be distributed as excess contributions under the ADP test, because these are required to be removed from participants' accounts. Next, in an effort to correct the ACP text, the employer will generally distribute any employee after-tax contributions, because these contributions have already been taxed as income to the employee. Finally, the employer will generally distribute (or forfeit) matching contributions until the test is corrected.

One important point should be understood with respect to corrective distributions and forfeitures. If the matching contributions that need to be corrected are not vested, they may not be distributed. Rather, the nonvested matching contributions must be forfeited. In contrast, any vested matching contribution must be distributed and may not be forfeited. There is one exception to this rule: vested matching contributions that were made along with distributed excess contributions (under the ADP test) must be forfeited to the degree necessary to avoid discriminatory availability problems, as discussed earlier in this chapter.

As with the ADP test corrections, there is a requirement for distributors of excess aggregate contributions to be so designated and made within twelve months of the end of the year in which the excess aggregate contributions were made. Similarly, the same 10 percent penalty tax to the employer applies to excess aggregate contributions that are not distributed within two-and-a-half months following the end of the year in which the contributions were made.

### Correcting By Means Of Additional Contributions

To correct excess aggregate contributions under the ACP test, the employer must contribute either matching contributions or QNECs. This process was discussed briefly earlier in discussing the correction of excess contributions under the ADP test.

## The Multiple-Use Test

The multiple-use test combined 401(k), after-tax, and employer-matching contributions for highly compensated employees and subjected them to a nondiscrimination test. The multiple-use test is repealed, effective for plan years beginning after December 31, 2001.

# SAFE HARBOR PLANS

Beginning in 1999, employers who sponsor a 401(k) plan have the option of designing the plan under one of two methods that will avoid the aforementioned complex annual nondiscrimination testing currently required. As most concepts related to tax qualified plans, safe harbor plans have their advantages and disadvantages and may not be the best option for all employers.

A safe harbor 401(k) plan will eliminate the ADP and ACP tests, provided the employer is willing to commit to a generous matching contribution or a non-elective contribution that will be made to all plan participants. In many cases, employers have currently been required to refund 401(k) contributions to all HCEs or have had to limit HCE deferrals in order to pass these tests. There are specific requirements that must be met in order for a plan to be considered a safe harbor. Specifically, the employer must meet one of the contributions requirements discussed below and satisfy the notice requirement to all employees.

## Contribution Requirements

The safe harbor contribution[62] that will meet both the ADP and ACP tests is: (1) a matching contribution of 100 percent of the employees' 401(k) deferrals up to three percent of compensation plus 50 percent of deferrals between three percent and five percent of compensation and match at any rate that the deferrals do not exceed six percent of an employee's compensation; or (2) a nonelective contribution of at least three percent of compensation to be made to all eligible employees and matching contributions are based on six percent of compensation and do not result in a rate of match for any HCE that is greater than the rate of match for a NHCE. Under the second option, a nonelective contribution of at least three percent of compensation to be made to all eligible employees alone would pass the ADP test.

An enhanced match is permitted, if such a match equals a total of contribution of at least the matching contribution that would have been required under the basic match formula, and that the rate of the enhanced match does not increase an employee's rate of contribution increases.

For example, if a participant chooses to defer five percent of compensation, the match under the basic formula would be four percent of compensation (100 percent of deferrals up to three percent plus an additional one percent, representing 50 percent of the deferrals between three percent and five percent). That means a matching contribution of 100 percent of deferrals up to four percent of compensation would satisfy the enhanced matching contribution formula.

## Eligibility

For either option, the compensation considered for the nonelective or matching contributions must be total compensation, up to the annual limit. The safe harbor contributions cannot be conditioned on any additional requirements, such as a participant completing 1,000 hours of service in the plan year or being employed on the last day of the plan year. However, the plan may still be designed to require service and age twenty-one as eligible requirements, and compensation can be limited to the portion of the plan year after which an employee has become eligible to participate.

Employer contributions under a safe harbor plan must always be fully vested and are subject to the same distribution restrictions as elective deferrals. Additionally, safe harbor contributions are not eligible for hardship distributions, even if the plan currently permits such distributions. Finally, the employer

---

62    IRS Notice 98-52.

must deposit the safe harbor matching contributions of the safe harbor nonelective contribution within twelve months after the close of the plan year.

## Required Contribution Specifications

Employers who wish to use a safe harbor plan design will need to amend their plan to specify which required contribution will be made. In a safe harbor plan, an employer can no longer wait until the end of a plan year to decide whether to make a discretionary contribution. Once the safe harbor contribution has been selected, it cannot be changed during the plan year.

## Notification

The other major requirement for a plan to be a safe harbor 401(k) plan is that participants must be notified in a timely manner before each plan year in which safe harbor contributions will be made. This notice must inform them as to whether of not a match or pro-rata nonelective contribution will be made, and must be provided before the date when an employee can participate. In this instance, the IRS has offered some relief from the general requirement that this notice be given at least 30 days, but not more than 90 days, before the beginning of the plan year.

Despite the fact that an employer with a safe harbor plan does not have the flexibility to change contribution rates or levels after the start of the plan year, IRS guidance does seem to permit the employer to make year to year amendments to alternate the safe harbor from the pro-rata contribution or match, or to remove the safe harbor entirely and have the plan return to traditional testing methods.

Finally, all 401(k) safe harbor plans must continue to allow employees the opportunity to change their elective deferral rates during the plan year. A reasonable opportunity to make such changes will be available if an employee has at least a 30-day grace period after the annual safe harbor notice to make any election changes.

# Chapter 6—PLAN ADMINISTRATION AND PARTICIPANT RECORD KEEPING

Plan administration and participant record keeping are two of the most vital elements in a 401(k) plan's operation and compliance. Plan administration is the consulting and regulatory compliance side of the plan. Participant record keeping is the process of maintaining participants' balances and records in the plan, including all activity relating to participants' accounts. Together, these two elements set a framework for the smooth operation of the plan.

## PLAN ADMINISTRATION

Although plan administration and participant record keeping are not the same functions, people in the industry often use these terms interchangeably. As a result, there is some confusion about whether any difference exists between the two. Thus, it is useful to understand the distinction. Participant record keeping is actually one subset of the overall plan administration function.

Essentially, plan administration includes the following responsibilities:

- Hiring plan attorneys, accountants, investment consultants, and actuaries, where necessary
- Determining eligibility, vesting, hardship cases, and other plan enforcement issues
- Advising participants of their rights and settlement options
- Directing distributions
- Preparing governmental reports and filings
- Preparing participant reports, records, loan amortizations and repayments, vesting records, and other participant information

# THE PLAN ADMINISTRATOR

ERISA requires every plan to designate a plan administrator, and absent such designation, ERISA considers the employer-sponsor to be the plan administrator. This is not the same thing as the common term plan administrator, which describes the person responsible for participant record keeping or actuarial functions. Such people, although performing administrative functions, are technically not plan administrators as defined under ERISA.

Many of the plan administrator's functions are discretionary determinations relating to claims for benefits. Most of these statutory responsibilities relate more accurately to defined benefit pension plans and have no specific application to defined contribution plans. ERISA, however, does not distinguish the definition of plan administrator depending on plan type. Moreover, it is clear that the plan administrator in a defined contribution plan such as a 401(k) plan still maintains a considerable degree of discretionary responsibility. Consequently, the plan administrator of any plan is deemed fiduciary by definition under ERISA section 3(21).

Under ERISA, the plan administrator may retain professional service providers to assist in the administration process. With respect to 401(k) plans, it is customary for outside parties to prepare the participant's records; work with the plan sponsor to develop enrollment and ongoing education materials as well as conduct enrollment meetings; prepare and file the required government filings; conduct the required discrimination testing; process participant distributions; and fulfill any other responsibility related to the operation of the plan.

# PARTICIPANT RECORD KEEPING

Participant record keeping takes different forms, as described later in this chapter. However, it is essentially the process of maintaining participants' balances and records in the plan. The plan administrator hires and works with the outside service provider who handles the participant record-keeping function.

Both plan administration and participant record keeping have undergone tremendous change during the last several years. Regulatory developments in defined-contribution plans, along with increased participant control over their investments, have forced the evolution of these functions and the technology that supports them.

Since the beginning of 401(k), the trend has been toward outsourcing plan administration and record keeping responsibilities. Plan sponsors hoping to reduce their own administrative burdens increasingly rely on both the resources and expertise of outside service providers. These service providers have responded to market demand with new products and technological innovations that we will discuss later in this chapter.

As part of this outsourcing trend and the need for greater levels of expertise, plan sponsors of mid-sized companies are turning to financial advisors to provide consulting services for the plan. In this consultant role, financial advisors select and monitor service providers, advise the plan sponsor on investment option choices, and provide communications/education support for the plan participants. Given the growing complexity of 401(k) plan administration, financial advisors offer invaluable support to plan sponsors of mid-sized companies in the fulfillment of their fiduciary responsibilities.

# MANAGING THE PLAN ADMINISTRATION AND RECORD-KEEPING PROCESS

It is critical to select quality service providers because the entire 401(k) plan operation depends on plan administration and record keeping.

## Choosing a Plan Administrator and Record Keeper

The administrative element of the plan is perhaps the most vital because it affects both the plan's operation and its ability to maintain its qualified status under the Internal Revenue Code and regulations. Thus, obtaining a plan administrator who is qualified to manage the plan is of paramount importance. Functioning much like a bandleader who coordinates and manages an entire orchestra, the plan administrator must identify any player that it out of tempo and quickly control the problem.

## Bundled Versus Unbundled Services

There are generally two ways to characterize 401(k) services: bundled and unbundled. Bundled services, which exist in several forms, generally are available through organizations that provide a complete package of investment, trustee, participant record keeping, and communication services. Arguably, the most efficient bundled arrangements are provided by one organization, such as a mutual fund company or a bank. This arrangement is frequently referred to as single-provider bundled services.

Bundled service arrangements have grown increasingly more popular as plan sponsors look to outsourcing more of their plan administration responsibilities. In fact, Access Research reports that regardless of plan size, plan sponsors overwhelmingly favor bundled service arrangements.[63] Among plans with fewer than 100 participants, 85 percent chose full service over unbundled arrangements for their 401(k) plans. Of plans that had between 100 and 1,000 participants, 78 percent chose full service and 22 percent chose unbundled arrangements. Finally, among plans with over 1,000 participants, 63 percent chose full service whereas 37 percent chose unbundled arrangements.

Single-provider bundled service arrangements are attractive because of the efficiencies created when one vendor serves in all areas. For example, bundled service providers can provide nondiscrimination testing and help educate participants about investing for retirement. Interactions among the different plan function areas are generally smoother because they are all linked electronically. Many service providers offering a bundled package have sophisticated technology to link investment management, trustee services, and record keeping, which enhances the efficiency and data sharing in plan operation. In addition, bundled service providers offer plan sponsors one point of contact that saves them multiple phone calls when trying to resolve any plan issues. Finally, according to Access Research, during the last five years the cost of record-keeping services per participant has been much more stable among bundled as opposed to unbundled service providers. Thus, the trend toward bundled service buying is driven in part by perceived cost efficiencies.

Employers with in-house benefit plan staff can work directly with the bundled service provider, helping to manage the entire plan's implementation, including the initiation of the required data transfer specifications. With contacts both inside the organization and with the service provider, there is greater opportunity for the plan to operate successfully, because the sponsor can, if the company wishes, interact with the different functional areas of the service provider. For example, if the sponsor's finance area wants significant involvement in investment option issues, the financial group can establish a relationship directly with the service provider's investment manager, in addition to the sponsor's usual contact person.

Companies that lack in-house expertise may want to hire a financial advisor to provide plan consulting services such as assistance in the selection of a service provider, implementation management, and service provider monitoring on an ongoing basis. The addition of a consultant for this type of organization can make the difference between a mediocre and a well-run plan, not to mention the management of fiduciary responsibility. Participation levels, deferral percentages, and the level of investment diversification among participants can measure a successful 401(k) plan. If these measures are successful, a plan will

---

63   Access Research, Inc., SPARK Marketplace Update (1996).

easily pass discrimination tests and participants will be able to rely upon their 401(k) plan for their retirement.

Bundled arrangements are available not only from large service providers but also can be created by separate large service providers who combine to create strategic alliances to offer these services. With the development of proper electronic data transfer systems, this type of arrangement can form a high-quality bundled service, because such an arrangement brings together superior talent in each plan component area. Prototypes for these multiple-vendor relationships based on strategic systems alliances exist today and will continue to be used in the future. These entail on-line (or live) feeds between the plan record keeper and the plan trustee. The trustee maintains an electronic link with the investment management organization. Because of these interfaces, the plan can function on a true daily basis with a record keeping system that is almost paperless. It is important to note that may traditional bundled service providers with their own family of funds can now incorporate investment options from other fund families into their record-keeping systems.

Evidently, the downside of some bundled arrangements is that they may lack flexibility with respect to required input and data from plan sponsors. For instance, they may require that the employer provide contribution data in a certain format that is incompatible with the plan sponsor's internal systems. In this case, the plan sponsor would have to adapt its system to meet the service provider's requirements.

In contrast, unbundled services generally refer to those arrangements in which the respective plan components are serviced by separate entities with no real relationship. There are still some organizations that represent themselves as bundled service providers although they are no more than unbundled arrangements in which the organization uses the back office of a plan administration or record-keeping firm.

In an automated environment with electronic data interchange (EDI), the unbundled arrangement functions much like a bundled arrangement. If, however, record keeping is performed in a manually processed environment, then it is a true unbundled arrangement. The same can be said of investment organizations that have their own record-keeping systems. If the system does not interface with the investment and trustee components of the plan, such an arrangement is an unbundled arrangement despite packaging and appearance that indicates the contrary.

The increased popularity of bundled over unbundled arrangements is largely a result of the growing trend among plan sponsors to outsource plan administration. Sponsors can now outsource plan administration. Sponsors can now outsource investment management, participant record keeping, trustee services, and even some monitoring of other vendors. For example, if a plan sponsor outsources its payroll function to a separate vendor, the bundled service provider can help manage the payroll vendor by setting up payroll tapes and backups directly with that vendor. Ultimately the bundled service provider can remove some of the sponsor's burden in dealing directly with a payroll vendor.

Current trends reflect a move toward total benefits outsourcing, in which a service provider takes on not only the plan administration and record-keeping functions of 401(k) plan but does the same for an organization's defined benefit and health and welfare plans. The goal is for plan participants to make one phone call to access their entire benefits package. Totally integrated benefits will enable participants to get information on and manage their 401(k), defined benefit, and health plans all from one resource. Systems and service development are in the works at some large service providers, who anticipate offering this service arrangement within the next few years.

Totally integrated benefits administration is driven by a need for the participant to have access to his or her entire financial picture in context. Therefore, participants need integrated information to make critical decisions that will affect their financial security because there is now a greater emphasis on both total financial planning and the need to save more. Plan sponsors need integrated information in order to manage properly the plan, as well as to determine what changes should be made in the overall benefit package for their participants.

## Defining Responsibilities

The key to successful 401(k) plan administration and record keeping is to properly define everyone's responsibilities. Individuals involved in plan administration and record keeping at both the plan sponsor and the service level must have a clear sense of their responsibilities, and a clear understanding of who their contact or support is on the other side of the relationship. This is particularly true for unbundled plans for which there are multiple service providers who may not have worked together previously. However, the same holds true for a bundled arrangement. For example, if the plan sponsor provides contribution information in a certain format to allow accurate processing by the service provider, the individuals who transmit this information must clearly understand their responsibility, so as not to break a processing cycle.

As most plan administrators can attest, plan record keeping is only as efficient or accurate as the data being provided. If an employer's system of providing contribution data is haphazard, late, or inaccurate, no amount of sophisticated plan record keeping will make the plan successful. Accurate and timely record-keeping systems begin with the employer and service provider setting expectations up front. The plan sponsor should take time early in the planning process to understand what the service provider needs to work out any record-keeping bugs in advance, and create a system that requires little or no human intervention. Often plan sponsors find the use of financial advisors or plan consultants useful to define the data layout and to set up the payroll-processing interface.

The service provider has an extremely important role in defining responsibilities and helping to create an efficient working relationship with the plan sponsor. The service provider must set expectations for the plan's needs from the plan sponsor but also be flexible enough to adapt their systems for receiving data to suit the plan sponsor's capabilities. One of the most useful approaches to creating a successful relationship is to put all responsibilities and expectations in writing.

Typically, a service agreement is executed between the plan sponsor and the service provider. As the foundation of the administrative relationship, this service agreement contains details on the various services for which the plan sponsor has contracted. In addition, the service agreement should contain performance standards by which to measure the provider's performance. For example, the agreement should include time standards for statements, loan processing, and distribution checks, as well as accuracy standards for financial transactions. Additional standards include speed of answer for telephone representatives, frequency of on-site visits by client officer personnel, and the level of support being provided for enrollment and ongoing education.

## Creating an Administrative Manual

No amount of automation will completely absolve the sponsor from responsibilities in the administration of the 401(k) plan, so putting all processes and responsibilities in writing has advantages for both the plan sponsor and service provider. For example, loan processing involves an element of employer judgment so a written procedure will dictate at what point and in which situations this judgment must be exercised. In addition, the employer involvement in administering the process of contributions from payroll demands a clear understanding on behalf of both the organization and the plan sponsor about when and where that involvement occurs. To optimize the plan's efficiency and minimize processing errors, all of these functions should be performed in a consistent manner pursuant to written standards.

Developing an administrative manual that describes the entire administration process, complete with periods and respective responsibilities, will help to maintain consistent administration. The administrative manual typically is the operations plan for the ongoing administration of the plan itself. Contained within the manual should be information regarding data transmission, procedures regarding withdrawals, loans, hardships, and so on. Because of the great amount of mobility in the workforce today, having a document that provides an institutional memory for all parties concerned is vital to the success of the plan. It should be the service provider's responsibility to create the manual from the outset of the relationship with the plan sponsor. The manual should also define systems requirements and reporting capabilities.

For a competent service provider, the administrative manual serves as a framework for successful administration as well as a series of commitments to the plan sponsor. As such, the manual can set expectations for service levels, and can be used as a tool to measure the quality of service provided. If the manual says that 98 percent of distribution checks must be mailed within a certain number of days, the service provider can measure actual performance against this standard and adjust procedures as necessary.

## Determining the Record Keeping System and Cycle

Although there are two types of record-keeping cycles—periodic and daily, during the past few years most plans have shifted to a daily record-keeping system, given its considerable advantages. Under a periodic record-keeping system, participants' accounts are valued according to a preestablished schedule, most commonly once every quarter.

With a quarterly system, participants receive benefit statements reflecting their account balances and any activity during the last quarter. However, because it normally takes four to six weeks after the end of the quarter for participants to receive their statements, they never really see the current value of their account. Further, participants in a periodic record-keeping system cannot make real-time investment transfers, because this type of system only allows them to make changes as of a certain date. This restriction can cause participants to make changes in their accounts at a time that may feel inappropriate, simply because it is their only option. Participants who want to make changes effective during a particular quarter cannot because their accounts must be valued before they can make transfers. If, as discussed earlier, the participants' account values are not determined until four to six weeks after the end of the quarter, it becomes impossible for the participants' instructions to be carried out in a timely manner.

The shift of investment control to participants during the last several years has mandated a shift to daily record-keeping systems, which enable participants to manage their accounts more effectively. In order to control truly their investment accounts, making changes when they deem appropriate, participants need timely, accurate information, and daily trading capabilities. Thus, there has been tremendous competitive pressure for organizations to develop systems that streamline the data flow, fully automate the record-keeping process, and provide participants with "on-demand" information.

Daily record-keeping systems offer daily valuation, daily processing, and daily transactions. Daily valuation means simply assigning a value to each participant's account on a daily basis, by multiplying the number of shares in each participant's account by the per-share price of the investments. On the other hand, daily processing means updating participant records and actually processing date received about contributions, investments, and distributions every day. Thus, the entire plan is balanced on a daily basis, such that all information is updated by the next business day. Accordingly, daily processing eliminates the need to wait until the end of a particular month or quarter to post transactions as is done with a periodic system.

Daily record keeping enables participants to execute investment changes, trigger distributions, and determine an account balance on a daily basis. Rather than work through their benefits office, participants can call the provider and make transactions directly, virtually twenty-four hours a day and seven days a week. In addition, daily record-keeping systems post transactions such as earnings, capital gains, and dividends immediately on receipt.

Daily systems are more equitable than periodic systems because they allow true daily accrual of earnings. This means that dividends will only be accrued in a participant's account, based on their individual accrual rate, which is determined by how long they have invested in a particular option. Under the old periodic systems, all participants simply earned a pro-rata share of dividends that were distributed at one point in time, regardless of when participants actually invested in the option. The same holds true in daily systems for distributions. Participant distributions are processed as they are requested, a more equitable approach than batch processing, which could cause participants to share in a gain or loss that occurred after they had actually requested the distribution.

Daily systems have necessitated innovations in—and a true commitment to—the technology that supports them. A critical part of these systems is the interface among a plan's record keeper, plan trustee, and investment manager to allow true data sharing among all parties. Such a system is most common among single-source bundled service providers, where the links among these three entities can be established internally. In addition, a true daily system requires a direct daily interface with a fund's purchase and sale system, which means an interface with a fund's transfer agent. This is a feature commonly seen with a bundled service provider where the transfer agent is in-house, or captive.

One of the main concerns with daily systems is the service provider's ability to offer daily valuation and pricing of outside investment options. Most plans use a variety of investment options for their 401(k) plans, some of which are more conducive to daily valuation.

- **Commingled Funds**
  For the most part, daily pricing is appropriate only with respect to commingled investment vehicles that can be reported with a per-share price, such as registered mutual funds, some bank collective funds, and insurance company separate accounts. Moreover, daily valuation of participants' accounts works best when the entire selection of investments within a given plan is limited to a single family of funds. Some innovations have been created whereby a single trust company is electronically tied to five or six different mutual fund families, but the best that such a system can provide is a two-day transaction turnaround time. The reason is that one fund group can never know the amount of proceeds after a redemption to be used in the purchase form another fund group.

- **Guaranteed Investment Contracts (GICs)**
  It is now possible to compute a daily price on most GICs, including commingled or pooled GIC funds, in which interest on the contracts is credited daily. However, not all service providers are capable of this service, nor do all GIC carriers cooperate. In general, GIC record keeping can be extremely complex, due to withdrawal provisions that vary widely from carrier to carrier. This is an area where an experienced service provider can often be of significant assistance in dealing with the plan's various GICs, and negotiating changes to the contracts that can facilitate plan administration. See Chapter 9 for further information on GICs.

- **Employer Securities**
  Another difficult asset to deal with in daily valued plans is employer stock that trades on a major exchange under three-day settlement rules. Although it is difficult to mix this investment with a mutual fund (whose system works on a next-day settlement system) for 401(k) plans, some record keepers have developed systems to do this, which will be discussed later on in this chapter.

- **Managed Accounts**
  Additionally, the use of independently managed accounts, although extremely popular in 401(k) plans, does not lend itself to a true daily system, because even if managed accounts are valued daily, they are not valued on a per-share basis; therefore, there must be some conversion program to combine these accounts with other daily valued vehicles.

- **Life Insurance and Real Estate**
  For obvious reasons, life insurance and real estate investments do not lend themselves to daily pricing.

Fortunately, some larger service providers have and will continue to develop more advanced technology to incorporate outside options such as GICs and other fund family options into their own daily systems.

## Valuation and Record Keeping of Employer Securities

Employer securities, such as company stock, present their own set of record-keeping challenges, particularly with respect to daily systems. In the past, the longer settlement rules for stock made it difficult to blend company stock with other mutual fund investments, but recently some service providers have developed sophisticated record-keeping systems to support both options.

The most efficient system for record-keeping company stock is one that provides share accounting rather than unit accounting. With share accounting, the participant owns shares of the company stock in his or her account, as opposed to units, which dilute the value of direct ownership because the unit valuation is actually a blend of the stock price and cash used to settle traces. More importantly, a participant can sell shares of company stock and buy shares of a mutual fund on the same day; the trade essentially washes "behind-the-scenes" because mutual fund companies can place a three-day settlement where they lock in the price of the stock today and pay for it in three days. With this type of system, the plan sponsor has the benefits of daily processing with the clarity of share accounting. Share accounting also provides a direct link for the participants to their own stock ownership. In other words, they can see the number of shares they own instantly, and plan sponsors strongly prefer that employees understand the extent of their investment in the company.

A service provider should be able to offer this type of record-keeping system for employer stock, as well as work with the sponsor to regulate volume stock trades, especially when making changes in the plan that impact market activity. Essentially, the service provider must recognize the importance of company stock as an option in the plan and work with the sponsor to manage it effectively.

## Daily Trading

Daily trading, which theoretically allows a participant to make investment changes on a given trading day, offers yet another way for participants to better manage their retirement savings accounts. Although the transaction is processed at the next available closing price of the investment option (generally the current day's price if before 4 PM or the next day's price if after 4 PM), the system still offers closer to "real-time" investing than would a periodic record-keeping system.

As daily trading had become more widespread over the past few years, many plan sponsors have had some fiduciary concerns with respect to allowing participants to trade their accounts so frequently. Their concern related to the risk that participants would "churn" their accounts, reacting too quickly to changing market conditions, which could hurt the performance of their accounts. However, according to Access Research, these concerns never actually materialized. Over a twelve-month period, participants increased their contribution rate and adjusted their allocation changes more frequently than making exchanges. For example, 77 percent of participants made no changes over a twelve-month period, 16.5 percent made one change, and only 6.3 percent made two or more exchanges. These statistics show no evidence of excessive trading activities. Instead, participant use of daily systems reflects a greater tendency toward inquiry and information gathering as opposed to transaction execution.[64] Further, plan sponsors recognize the need to allow participants to make timely investment transfers, according to their own needs and investment goals.

Further, participants who transfer out of a mutual fund based investment option within months, or even years, of purchasing them are increasingly paying a higher price to get out, particularly if the funds invest overseas or in a single sector, according to a new study.

The Boston-based Financial Research Corp. found the number of funds charging redemption fees rose 82 percent between December 31, 1999 and March 30, 2001.[65] Redemption fees are collected from participants who transfer out of fund shares before a specified period, usually ranging from a few months to several years. The charge, an average 1.13 percent of the sales transaction, according to the FRC data, is designed to discourage investors from making short-term investments in funds.

As a final option, sponsors do have the option within a daily trading system to limit the number of exchanges participants make. For example, sponsors could allow participants to make one change every three months, but at any time within that period. Another viable solution would be to allow participants four exchanges as part of a standard package and charge them transaction fees for any changes in excess of the four.

---

64  Access Research, Inc., SPARK Marketplace Update (1996).
65  Lisa Singhania, Mutual fund redemption fees are rising, USA TODAY (July 12, 2001).

## Participant Services by Internet and Telephone

The most frequently cited reason for using a daily system is to provide a mechanism whereby participants can directly initiate changes or obtain information/education about their accounts. To this end, service providers have developed sophisticated telephone services to offload this responsibility from the plan sponsor.

Telephone services may be available both through live representatives and through an automated voice response system or speak to a representative to request investment literature, make investment changes, check account balances, change contribution levels, and initiate loans and withdrawals. Representatives may offer further assistance with respect to problem resolution and helping participants determine suitable investment options.

Most plan sponsors are concerned with the telephone representatives' knowledge of their plan. As such, these representatives should have a thorough understanding of plan provisions so they can offer adequate assistance to the participants that speak to them. Updated record-keeping technology now puts plan provisions and details online and at the representatives' fingertips to help them respond to participant inquiries.

Voice response system technology has undergone tremendous development as more organizations look to outsource their participant servicing. Through a voice response system, participants can obtain daily balances, loan and withdrawal information, and literature requests. This technology also enables participants to initiate investment exchanges, change contribution allocations, get performance information, model loan amortization schedules, and actually initiate the loan process by printing and mailing (or faxing) to the employee signature-ready loan documents.

Because a voice response system eliminates the need for live representatives around the clock, it offers significant cost savings that the service provider can pass along to the plan sponsor. In fact, voice response systems have become such an accepted way to handle participant servicing that many service providers report that roughly 60 to 70 percent of participant calls go to voice response while only 30 to 40 percent go to representatives.

## Record Keeping Technology: Today and Tomorrow

More sophisticated record-keeping technology available today has much to offer plan sponsors wishing to outsource more of their record-keeping functions. The entire record-keeping function is undergoing a metamorphosis from paper to paperless, and the more advanced the electronic capabilities become, the more these systems can reduce plan sponsors' burdens.

Record-keeping technology today has few paper requirements left, except for certain legal requirements with respect to loans and hardship withdrawals. Payroll processing that previously involved cumbersome paperwork can now be done via electronic transmission directly from plan sponsors to their service providers. Even plan documents and service agreements can be stored electronically, thus reducing storage space, making document retrieval and revision much more efficient, and ultimately reducing the cost to the plan sponsor.

The most advanced record-keeping systems use rules-based technology, which allows them to customize software to a particular plan's provisions, such that all transactions pass through a front-end system of checks and balances. For example, if a participant calls to make a telephone exchange, and has already used up a limited number of exchanges set by his or her plan, the rules-based technology would not allow the transaction to be processed. The rules-based system programs seek to eliminate the opportunity for errors to occur during front-end processing.

Another advancement in record-keeping systems is imaging technology, which can take all written participant correspondence, file it permanently on optical disc, and pull it up on screen to use for participant inquiries and transactions. Imaging technology offers a means of maximizing the efficiency of paper by using technology coupled with comprehensive back-end reporting, which not only reduces processing errors but also maximizes use of the data in the system.

Looking ahead to the next five years, record-keeping and plan administration functions will become more automated and integrated, and, driven by market demand, will respond to information requests more quickly and accurately. Indeed, the goal of most of new technology will be to produce information in an integrated, on-demand fashion.

The challenge for service providers is to develop technology that can be customized to fit the needs of many types of plans. As there is no single standard 401(k) product, it is virtually impossible to meet plan sponsor requirements with one off-the-shelf piece of technology. These market-driven technological innovations will also require buy-in from plan sponsors because they to will need to commit some resources toward the development of integrated information systems. Plan sponsors will most likely need to change the way they transmit information electronically, in order to fit the requirements of updated service provider technology. Service providers must therefore take a more proactive, consultative approach to systems development, educating the plan sponsors not only about new requirements but more importantly about the need for them to commit resources (staff, time) toward the common end of a more cost-effective, integrated record-keeping system.

To meet the on-demand information requirements of the 401(k) plan market, service providers are making plan information available and interactive through a variety of media, including the Internet. In the best case, technology developments in 401(k) plan record keeping over the next five years will result in more accurate and immediate information available on a customized basis. For example, plan sponsors will have access to better, more concise financial reports in more standardized formats. Service providers are currently developing systems to offer plan sponsors greater flexibility to manage plan data and format it to meet their current and future needs.

## TRUSTEE SERVICES

Every plan must have a trustee. Because the trustee provides such a critical communications function, the most efficient arrangement is to obtain trustee services through a bundled service provider. The trustee must take information from the plan's investments and match it to the participant records. This process is greatly facilitated when both are handled under one roof. The trustee will also handle company stock certificates and any "in-kind" distributions to participants. In addition, the trustee will interface with GIC providers or any outside fund families.

The trustee arrangement is formally established through a trust agreement, which outlines the obligations of both the trustee and the plan sponsor with respect to any areas falling under trustee services. These trust arrangements are nondiscretionary so that the plan fiduciaries retain full responsibility for voting company stock and making decisions with respect to the plan's investment options. As such, this is a purely administrative trust relationship.

## REPORTING AND DISCLOSURE REQUIREMENTS

Like other qualified plans, 401(k) plans are subject to extensive reporting and disclosure requirements. Normally, the plan administrator handles this function; although some plan sponsors choose to handle this responsibility internally or to have their tax advisors handle it. Plan sponsors should also expect support from their service providers, particularly with respect to preparing government filings.

Because these requirements have been dealt with at length in many other works, they are not covered in any detail here. Rather, this chapter simply describes these various requirements in basic terms and refers readers to more comprehensive sources.

# REPORTING TO GOVERNMENT AGENCIES

## Summary Plan Description
Under ERISA, the 401(k) plan administrator is required to file with the DOL a document called a summary plan description (SPD) as well as a document called a summary of material modifications (SMM). Both of these documents are used as basic reference tools for employees to understand the provisions of their plan, as well as their rights. Each of these documents has specific content requirements that are covered in more detail in Chapter 10.

## Form 5500 and Related Documents
All plans must file an annual report, the IRS Form 5500, with the IRS and the DOL. A number of different 5500 forms might apply to a given plan, depending on the size of the participant base, ad corporate structure. In addition, a variety of different schedules might be required, depending on the features of the plan. The process of completing Form 5500 is burdensome and requires a great deal of expertise in pension and tax law. In fact, some of the required schedules must be audited and certified by an independent public accountant.

For these reasons, plan sponsors should seriously consider retaining competent professionals to complete this form and related schedules. Competent service providers, as well as brokers and advisors, have considerable expertise in the preparation of the 5500 forms and can provide invaluable support in the completion of this reporting requirement.

## Form W-2
Whenever a participant receives a payment from the plan in any year, the plan administrator must report such payments to the IRS and the Social Security Administration by filing a Form W-2 for related to each specific employee. In addition, the employee receiving the distribution must receive a copy of the Form W-2. Ideally, the trustee who has dispersed the funds should handle this function. Such a trustee should be familiar with the general filing requirements pertaining to Form W-2.

## Form 1099-R
Under the revised Form 1099-R, all distributions from a plan must be reported to the IRS. Again, a competent trustee should be fully capable of performing this function.

## SEC Form S-8
The SEC Registration Statement should be filed on 401(k) plans offering employer securities as an investment option.

**IRS Form 5300**

A determination letter request, Form 5300, is where a plan sponsor asks, however is not required, the IRS to review and approve the form of its plan document.

# NONDISCRIMINATION TESTING

401(k) plans are subject to comprehensive and detailed regulations requiring, in essence, the fair application of benefits to all eligible employees. Section 410(b) of the Internal Revenue Code requires that to be qualified, a 401(k) plan must cover a nondiscriminatory group of employees. These regulations are dealt with in Chapter 5.

# CHANGING SERVICE PROVIDERS: THE CONVERSION PROCESS

According to an Investment Company Institute (ICI) research report, more than 70 percent of plan sponsors planning to switch providers cited "dissatisfaction with service" as their impetus for making a change. Some of the service issues mentioned were participant services, timeliness of participant statements, and the accuracy of record keeping.[66]

Once a plan sponsor decides to switch providers, the conversion process must be carefully mapped out, with commitment to timelines and milestones on both the part of the plan sponsor and the new provider. Perhaps the most important issue with respect to a conversion is the length of time to completion, which depends on the size and complexity of the plan. Most conversions take from four to six months for completion.

Another important factor in the conversion process is the manner in which investments will be handled at the new provider. If plan sponsors want to keep participant assets invested in the market, rather than selling to cash for the transition, they can map over the accounts to similar funds at the new provider. Finally, plan sponsors should decide whether they want to do a reenrollment in the new plan. In other words, offer the participants new fund choices once the plan moves to the new provider.

Agreement on certain milestones is paramount to a successful conversion, including (1) the date on which the last valuation will be calculated by the old provider; (2) the date on which the telephone and Internet services at the new provider go "live"; and (3) the point at which the new provider can start accepting new contributions.

---

66   Investment Company Institute, ICI Research Report, Winter 1995.

## Conversion Milestones

Following are the important processes that characterize plan conversions:

- **Implementation meeting**—This is essentially a "kickoff" meeting during which the service provider and plan sponsor meet to reconfirm plan provisions and how the plan will operate. In addition, there should be a discussion of any plan document changes that might be necessary before final implementation of the plan. The service provider should present a conversion schedule and overview of administrative procedures, identifying all responsibilities at each step. This meeting is also used to introduce key players in the process, including the individuals who will support the plan sponsor during the enrollment period. Finally, the implementation meeting serves to confirm plan sponsor expectations of how the 401(k) plan services will be delivered.

- **Enrollment**—During the enrollment period, the plan sponsor and service provider work together to create the enrollment materials that will explain plan provisions, features, and benefits, as well as provide employees with the necessary forms to join the plan. Depending on the plan's particular needs, enrollment materials may be standard off-the-shelf pieces or customized. Enrollment periods typically last from three to four weeks, during which enrollment meetings are held to introduce or educate employees about the plan, its investments, and the benefits of saving for retirement.

- **Last valuation**—The prior record keeper completes the final update of participant and plan records before the plan's assets are transferred to the new record keeper on this date.

- **Test conversion**—Before actually receiving the assets from the old record keeper, the new service provider should test the conversion data by loading some plan information up on its own system. The test ensures that the information will flow through correctly, as delivered by the old provider, on the new provider's record keeping system.

- **Asset transfer**—At this point, all assets are liquidated from the old record keeper and are wired to the new provider. Typically, the plan's assets are invested ("mapped") into similar vehicles offered by the new provider. The new provider should begin processing and investing all contributions, while balancing the assets that have just been transferred. There is typically a blackout period following asset transfer during which distributions cannot be processed unless circumstances mandate an exception

- **Final data received**—The new provider receives final records from the prior record keeper.

- **Participant balances loaded**—The new provider posts all data to the system, including balances and historical information. At this time, all reconciliation work should be completed, and all accounts should be made current with earnings/losses. Finally, reallocations of participant accounts, if applicable, are processed.

- **Live phone and Internet service**—Participants have full access to their accounts, including the ability to transfer balances. The blackout period is now complete and all transactions should now be available to participants.

The most successful conversions involve an ongoing dialogue between the plan sponsor and the service provider(s), from implementation through employee education. Setting expectations up front will help to ensure satisfaction at the end of the conversion for both the new service provider and the plan sponsor.

# SARBANES-OXLEY ACT NOTICE

The U.S. Department of Labor (DOL) has finalized, with some changes, requirements for blackout notices to 401(k) plan participants as required by the Sarbanes-Oxley Act.[67] The guidance addresses the required contents and timing of the notice, and includes a model notice.

### Blackout Notice Requirements—In General

A blackout is defined generally as a temporary suspension, limitation or restriction of participants' or beneficiaries' rights otherwise available under the plan to diversify or direct investments, or obtain a loan or distribution. Plan administrators must meet the notice requirements whenever a blackout will last for three consecutive business days or more.

---

67    Sarbanes-Oxley Act of 2002 was primarily intended to address fraud in financial reporting and lack of oversight by self-interested senior corporate management; however, it modifies the reporting requirements under Section 16 of the Exchange Act, and restricts the purchase and sales of executive officers and directors during any blackout period.

## Contents of Notice

Concerning the contents of the notice, the guidance indicates the following:

- The notice must describe the reasons for the blackout period, and the participants' and beneficiary's rights' that will be suspended, limited or restricted.

- The notice must indicate the blackout period's projected duration. Previous guidance had required plan administrators to identify the expected start and end dates. Under the final guidance, however, plan administrators may instead identify the calendar week during which the blackout period will begin and end, provided that during such weeks information as to whether the blackout period has begun or ended is readily available, without charge, such as via a toll-free number or Web site, and the notice describes how to access the information.

- In the case of investments affected, the notice must state that participants and beneficiaries should evaluate the appropriateness of their current investment decisions in light of their inability to direct or diversify their assets during the blackout period.

- The notice must provide the name, address and phone number of the plan administrator or other contact responsible for answering participants' questions about the blackout.

## Timing of Notice

If plan administrators do not issue notice of the blackout period at least thirty days before it begins, in most cases the notice must explain the delay. The notice may not be issued more than sixty days before the blackout, although plan administrators may provide supplemental communication to participants before then.

The thirty-day advance notice requirement does not apply under three circumstances:

- When deferring the blackout period for thirty days after giving the notice would violate ERISA's fiduciary standards (e.g., if the plan fiduciary immediately suspends investment in employer stock because the employer has filed for bankruptcy)

- When the events prompting the blackout were unforeseeable or beyond the plan administrator's control

- When the blackout period applies only to one or more participants or beneficiaries solely in connection with their becoming, or ceasing to be, participants or beneficiaries of the plan as a result of a merger, acquisition, divestiture or similar transaction involving the plan or plan sponsor

In each of these circumstances, the plan administrator must furnish the notice to all affected participants and beneficiaries, as soon as reasonably possible under the circumstances, unless such notice in advance of the termination of the blackout period is impracticable.

## Updated Notice
If the duration of a blackout period changes after notice is provided, the administrator must issue an updated notice to all affected participants and beneficiaries explaining the reasons for the change and identifying all material changes to the previous notice. The administrator must furnish the updated notice as soon as reasonably possible, unless such notice in advance of the termination of the blackout period is impracticable.

## Exclusions from Blackout Period Definition
A blackout period does not include a suspension, limitation, or restriction under the following conditions:

- Results from application of the securities laws
- Is a regularly scheduled suspension, limitation or restriction under the plan (or change thereto), provided it has been disclosed to affected plan participants and beneficiaries through at least one of the following:
  - o The summary plan description
  - o A summary of material modifications
  - o Materials describing specific investment alternatives under the plan and limits thereon or any changes thereto
  - o Participation or enrollment forms any other documents and instruments under which the plan was established or operates that have been furnished to such participants and beneficiaries
- Occurs due to a qualified domestic relations order or a pending determination of whether a domestic relations order already filed with the plan (or reasonably anticipated to be filed) is a qualified order
- Occurs due to a participant's action or inaction, or because of an action or claim by a party unrelated to the plan involving a participant's account

## Penalties

The penalty for violations is $100 per participant per day, which means that a plan with 1,000 participants that has a fourteen-day blackout period but fails to give timely notice may be penalized $1.4 million.

Given the enormity of the potential penalty amounts, employers—even those not planning a blackout period—should review their plan operations, keeping in mind the exclusion from the blackout period definition for any regularly scheduled suspension, limitation or restriction already adequately disclosed to affected plan participants and beneficiaries. If adequate disclosure has not been made, employers should do so as soon as possible.

## Notice to Issuer of Employer Securities

Plan administrators also must furnish notice to the issuer of any employer securities held by the plan and subject to the blackout period. If the duration of the blackout period specified in the notice changes, the plan administrator must furnish an updated notice to the employer. Notice to the agent for service of legal process for the employer will constitute notice to the employer, unless the employer informs the plan administrator that someone else should receive notice. If the employer designates the plan administrator as the person to receive notice, the employer will be deemed to have received notice when the notice is furnished to affected participants and beneficiaries.

This notice to the employer relates to another provision in Sarbanes-Oxley that bans company insiders from buying or selling certain employer stock during certain blackout periods, even stock held outside the 401(k) plan. To facilitate this ban, the employer must provide notice to the affected executives and the Securities and Exchange Commission, under commission rules.

# Chapter 7—FIDUCIARY RESPONSIBILITY AS APPLIED TO 401(k) PLANS

The central purpose of ERISA is to protect the benefits and rights of participants and the beneficiaries. All IRS-qualified plans are regulated by ERISA, which imposes significant fiduciary responsibilities on plan managers and sponsors. Under ERISA, plan sponsors are required to act with care, skill, prudence, and diligence in the best interests of participants and beneficiaries. In the current complex regulatory and investment environment, satisfying the fiduciary responsibility provisions of ERISA is more difficult than ever.

## WHAT EVERY PERSON INVOLVED WITH 401(k) PLANS NEEDS TO KNOW

Many people involved with overseeing 401(k) plans fail to understand that they are subject to the same fiduciary responsibility provisions as for any other type of qualified plan.[68] Accordingly, a multitude of people associated with the plan may be making decisions or otherwise acting in a way that could raise an issue of personal or corporate liability. This liability might arise because of inadvertent or careless conduct with respect to the 401(k) plan. The vehicle giving rise to such liability will be the fiduciary responsibility provisions under ERISA.

Anyone having any relationship with respect to a 401(k) plan needs to have a basic familiarity with the fiduciary responsibility provisions of ERISA. Even if just to establish sensitivity for the types of conduct that might give rise to claims of liability, these people need to be aware. In recent years, the frequency of litigation over the issue of fiduciary violations has increased dramatically. People whose functions once were thought ministerial in nature suddenly find themselves on the defense of claims by disgruntled plan participants as well as the U.S. Department of Labor.

---

68  Eileen Hess, It's a Dangerous Time to be a Fiduciary (March 1, 2003).

One purpose of this chapter is to set forth the minimum rules governing the conduct of the fiduciaries that run the 401(k) plan. A second purpose is to illustrate the unresolved issues in the area of fiduciary responsibility as it pertains to participant-directed 401(k) plans. The final purpose is to describe who is a fiduciary under ERISA because any finding of liability depends on a finding that the people who are faulted acted in a fiduciary capacity to the plan.

## Participant-Directed Plans

At the outset of this discussion dealing with fiduciary responsibility under ERISA and how these provisions apply to self-directed 401(k) plans, it is useful to draw several distinctions. First, as is discussed throughout this chapter, the majority of 401(k) plans today are structured to give employees some measure of control over how their money is invested in the plan. These plans are set up in an effort to be treated as participant-directed or self-directed plans. These terms are often used interchangeably throughout this chapter.

Participant-directed plans are useful for a number of reasons. First, they enable employees to make their own investment decisions and thereby offer employees a greater feeling of control over their retirement savings. In addition participant-directed plans, if properly structured and administered, offer some measure of insulation to plan fiduciaries with regard to the ultimate investment allocations made by participants in their individual accounts. This theory holds that if an employee is given the power to allocate his or her own account between several investment options according to his or her own wishes, there is no reason to hold some other person responsible for how the employee chooses to allocate the account. Unfortunately, as will be discussed, this theory is subject to some wrinkles.

Despite the protections offered by participant-directed plans, they raise as many unresolved issues as they solve. As discussed later, for an ordinary employer-directed plan, in which the plan fiduciaries make the investment decisions with regard to the entire portfolio, it is straightforward to determine what to do to stay within the bounds of ERISA's fiduciary structure. This is not to say that doing so is easy; rather, it means that there is considerable guidance available to trustees through DOL interpretations, court decisions, and public commentary to allow trustees to make these decisions within an established framework. Hence, employer-directed plan fiduciary responsibilities are somewhat less ambiguous than participant-directed plans.

To the contrary, the same cannot be said with regard to participant-directed plans. Although it appears that there is some measure of reduced responsibility for the investment allocation decisions in these plans, the argument can be made that this was not a big problem in the first instance. A prudently managed employer-directed 401(k) plan would not place participants in a position to claim fiduciary breaches.

Furthermore, by placing investment authority in the hands of employees, plan fiduciaries create responsibilities that they never had before, particularly in the area of participant communications. Once a plan gives employees this substantial investment power, the obligation to educate and inform participants increases dramatically. Recent lawsuits have been brought by participants in participant-directed plans who were not given enough information to exercise this substantial responsibility.[69]

One of the biggest problems facing 401(k) plan fiduciaries of participant-directed plans is that this obligation to inform cannot be estimated. There is little guidance in the nature of regulations or case law for plan fiduciaries to look. This chapter will attempt define standards; nevertheless, in reality these are nothing more than commonsense solutions. Eventually, these standards will be created as they always are: in the courts, at the expense of plan fiduciaries. Thus, many of today's well-meaning plan fiduciaries may find themselves liable because they could not determine how far to go in informing participants about the investment selections in the plan.

Finally, the fact that a plan is participant-directed does not relieve the 401(k) plan fiduciary from any and all other fiduciary responsibility for the plan. Rather, such a setup simply relieves the fiduciary of the responsibility for asset allocation in participants' accounts. Thus, the extent of benefits achieved by offering a self-directed plan is questionable when weighed against the unknown fiduciary risks.

Above all, there is no mandate that 401(k) plans be participant-directed; this is optional. Thus, given the fact that the protections offered to plan fiduciaries are marginal at best, the reason that the majority of 401(k) plans are moving in the direction of participant direction is twofold:

- Having already given this power to employees, it would be nearly impossible to revert to employer-directed plans. Employees overall would never accept this result; they have become used to it and view it as their right, rather than a privilege.

- Perhaps more importantly, plan fiduciaries are overall mistaken about the true nature of the protections offered to them in a participant-directed plan under section 404(c).

---

69    Tittle v. Enron Corp., 284 F.Supp.2d 511 (S.D. Tex. 2003); In re WorldCom, Inc. ERISA Litigation.

Unless 401(k) plan sponsors as a group gain a more refined understanding of the entire landscape of ERISA's fiduciary responsibility provisions and the limited, though useful, protections offered under section 404(c), it is possible that today's decisions could actually increase (rather than decrease) potential fiduciary liability among 401(k) plan fiduciaries. These thoughts will be explored in depth throughout this chapter.

## Employer-Directed Plans

As noted earlier, so-called employer-directed plans (also known as trustee-directed plans) differ from participant-directed plans insofar as the investment decisions are made uniformly for all participants by either a plan fiduciary or an investment committee. Today, although most 401(k) plans attempt to be participant-directed, the majority of other non-401(k)-defined contribution plans are employer-directed (even though they are permitted to be participant-directed).[70] Noticeably, there is a greater measure of predictability in employer-directed plans about what the fiduciary responsibilities are with respect to the management of plan assets and their obligation to communicate to employees.

Besides the normal fiduciary obligations discussed later, the practical risk to plan fiduciaries in maintaining an employer-directed plan is that participants will second guess the fiduciaries' investment judgment, either that it was too conservative or too aggressive to be prudent under ERISA. Plan fiduciaries that are well informed about their responsibilities should be able to live with this risk. Prudent management and common sense, combined with an understanding of the landscape in which trustees operate, offer the best protections.

# THE BASIC FIDUCIARY RESPONSIBILITIES

## Overview and History

As noted earlier, 401(k) plans, as qualified plans, are subject to the extensive fiduciary responsibility provisions that apply to qualified plans generally. However, because of the presence of employee contributions, and the likelihood that participants will have some say in the investment decisions respecting the management of their individual accounts, 401(k) plans are generally fraught with more potential for fiduciary pitfalls. As a result, people associated with the management of the 401(k) plan need to be aware of the overall

---

70  Fundamentals of Employee Benefit Programs, Fifth Edition, Employee Benefit Research Institute, 1997.

responsibilities as they relate to the plan, as well as some sensible ways to manage these substantial responsibilities.

In its most basic terms, ERISA section 404(a) directs fiduciaries of all plans to act solely in the interest of the plan's participants and beneficiaries and for the exclusive purpose of providing benefits for these people. Further, a fiduciary must act prudently, diversify the investment of plan assets, and generally act in a manner consistent with plan documents.

In addition to this general requirement, plan fiduciaries are subject to the prudent man standard of care. This standard requires a fiduciary to act "with the care, skill, prudence, and diligence under the circumstances then prevailing that a prudent man acting in a like capacity and familiar with such matters would use..."[71]

With these standards, there is little mystery why plan fiduciaries can become confused about the scope of their responsibilities under ERISA. This nebulous standard forms the foundation of ERISA's fiduciary responsibility provisions that control the conduct of all plan fiduciaries. It is from this language, as well as the legislative history of ERISA, that the DOL and the courts have fashioned a body of law governing the conduct of plan fiduciaries. In view of the fact that this language is so open-ended, it is easy to see how plan fiduciaries might be nervous about how their investment decisions might be interpreted after the fact.

The legislative history of ERISA shows that Congress intended to incorporate the core principles of fiduciary responsibility as they developed in the common law of trusts.[72] These common law rules date back hundreds of years and govern the relationship that a common law trustee has to the beneficiary of the trust. It was on these principles that Judge Samuel Putnam formulated the Prudent Man Rule in 1830.[73] In enacting ERISA, Congress borrowed the prudent man rule. Thus, courts interpreting ERISA have found it useful and practical to draw on these common law principles in deciding fiduciary questions under ERISA.

---

71   ERISA §404(a)(1).

72   Michael S. Gordon, Overview: Why Was ERISA Enacted?, in The Employee Retirement Income Security Act of 1974: The First Decade 6-24 (U. S. Senate, Special Com. on Aging) (1984).

73   Harvard College v. Amory, 26 Mass. (9 Pick.) 446, 461.

Interestingly, however, Congress specifically noted that the common law fiduciary standards were not to be applied automatically to employee benefit plans; rather they were to be applied "bearing in mind the specific nature and purpose of employee benefit plans."[74] Thus, the rigid rules of the common law are generally not to be incorporated reflexively under ERISA; rather they are to be drawn on by courts in fashioning analogous principles.

From these rigorous principles, developed over hundreds of years in the common law, has evolved the fiduciary responsibility body of law under ERISA. This body of law is still in its evolution stages, which suggests why it is so difficult for plan fiduciaries to properly gauge whether their conduct is always permissible under the statute. Therefore, fiduciaries today should have at least learned that there is no bright line test for determining whether a given action is permissible because any decision can always be reviewed and second-guessed.

Nowhere in the fiduciary body of law are there more developments than in the area of participant-directed 401(k) plans. As of the publication of this book, several cases raise questions regarding aspects of participant-directed 401(k) features. As a result, plan fiduciaries are left with little guidance about how they should proceed to manage their fiduciary responsibility in these plans, where the likelihood for employee dissatisfaction runs higher than in any other type of plan. Accordingly, plan fiduciaries must be especially careful in determining how they will proceed with these plans.

Finally, one cannot exaggerate the significance of the fiduciary responsibility provisions, particularly about how they relate to 401(k) plans. This fiduciary duty is perhaps more stringent and less understood than any standard ordinarily applied in normal financial matters. This industry is at the threshold of developing content for this standard. Nowhere is this more accurate than in the area of 401(k) plans. Today's decisions and actions will dictate tomorrow's potential liability. Plan fiduciaries have in their own hands the power to manage this liability.

---

74  Varity Corp. v. Howe, 116 S. Ct. 1065 (1996); See ERISA §2(a); See also H. R. Rep. No. 93-533, supra, at 3-5, 11-13, 2 Leg. Hist. 2350-2352; 2358-2360; H. R. Conf. Rep. No. 93-1280, pp. 295, 302 (1974), 3 Leg. Hist. 4562, 4569.

Figure 7-1: Fiduciary Duties of ERISA Applied to 401(k) Plans

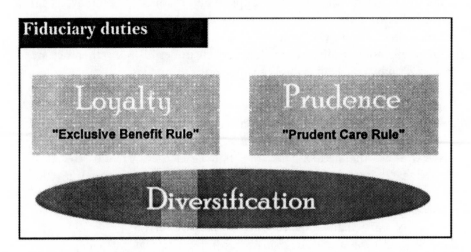

## The Exclusive Benefit Rule

Under section 404(a)(1)(A) of ERISA, a fiduciary of a plan must discharge his or her investment duties for the exclusive purpose of providing benefits to participants and beneficiaries. Courts have taken a narrow view of this provision, requiring that any action with respect to the investment or expenditure of plan assets be made with the sole purpose of benefiting participants and beneficiaries. Although the Exclusive Benefit Rule is phrased in terms of "never," "solely," and "exclusively," the courts have recognized that a literal reading of the statute is nonsensical and have readily acknowledged that incidental benefits may flow to the fiduciary or the plan sponsor as long as the fiduciary's primary motivation is to benefit the plan.[75] This rule in essence conveys a duty of loyalty.

In the case of 401(k) plans, one of the more apparent risks of violating this provision would be in decisions that are made because of business objectives or priorities. For instance, the decision to hire a commercial bank as the investment adviser to the plan in exchange for a favorable interest rate on business loans or more favorable terms for a line of credit would violate ERISA's exclusive purpose rule.

---

75   ERISA §404(a)(1)(A).

# The Prudent Man Rule

Under section 404(a)(1)(B) of ERISA, a fiduciary of the plan must discharge "his or her duties…with the care, skill prudence, and diligence under the circumstances then prevailing that a prudent man acting in a like capacity and familiar with such matters would use in the conduct of an enterprise of a like character and with like aims."

Although this rule is referred to under the common law as the prudent man rule, within the context of ERISA, this rule is commonly known in the industry as the prudent expert rule. The reason for this is that courts and the DOL have interpreted fiduciaries' actions by incorporating a standard of what an investment expert would do in similar circumstances.

In attempting to fulfill these responsibilities, fiduciaries should bear in mind certain principles that have been set forth by courts applying these fiduciary rules in real-world situations:[76]

1. **A fiduciary's lack of familiarity with investments is no excuse.** Under an objective standard, fiduciaries are to be judged according to others acting in like capacity and familiar with such matters. This means that plan fiduciaries are held to a standard of a prudent fiduciary with experience. Plan fiduciaries may not blindly make investment decisions or blindly rely on others; they must make decisions within a meticulous framework.

2. **The standard is not of a prudent layperson but that of a prudent fiduciary who has experience dealing with similar situations.** It is not sufficient that a plan fiduciary act prudently in their mind. Instead, that person must act prudently by comparison with a standard based on an experienced professional fiduciary. Thus, where the fiduciary lacks this experience, there is an affirmative obligation to seek independent advice.

3. **The test of prudence focuses on the fiduciary's conduct in investigating, evaluating, and making the investment.** In other words, the fiduciary's independent investigation of the merits of a particular investment is at the heart of the prudent man standard. A fiduciary engages in deciding to hire a particular investment advisor that becomes central to his or her fulfillment of ERISA's fiduciary responsibility provisions in the process.

4. **A fiduciary has an affirmative obligation to seek independent advice when he or she lacks the requisite education, experience, and skill, and must go to great lengths to establish a record for his or her actions.**

---

76 See Katsaros v. Cody, 744 F.2d. 170 (2d Cir. 1994); United States v. Mason Tenders Dist. Council of Greater New York, 909 F Supp. 882, 886 (SD NY 1995).

When selecting a professional investment manager to manage all or a piece of a plan's portfolio, a fiduciary has an obligation to seek the advice of independent consultants. The failure to make any independent investigation and evaluation of a potential plan investment is in and of itself a breach of fiduciary obligations.

5. **The plan fiduciary maintains the fiduciary obligation to monitor the performance of that manager and to take corrective action if necessary.** Even after the selection of the investment advisor, the plan fiduciary must monitor the performance of that advisor. The plan fiduciary is not permitted to ignore the plan after the delegation has been made; rather, the plan fiduciary should be monitoring the investments on an ongoing basis by reference to an objective and relevant series of indexes.

ERISA section 402(c)(2) permits either a named fiduciary or a fiduciary designated by a named fiduciary to employ others for the purpose of rendering advice regarding any responsibility the fiduciary has under the plan. Section 401(c)(3) further permits the named fiduciary to appoint an investment manager or managers to manage the assets of the plan. When this appointment is properly made, the plan fiduciaries are not liable for the acts and omissions of the investment manager. It has been well established that the decision to hire an investment manager to manage assets of a plan is a fiduciary decision in and of itself that requires the application of ERISA's prudence requirements.

In this regard, the DOL has supported guidelines that may be followed in a prudent selection of a person or entity to invest ERISA plan assets.[77] These guidelines, which are also examples of common sense, would require a plan fiduciary to do the following:

- Evaluate the person's or organizations' qualifications:
    - o   The expertise in the particular area of investments under consideration and with other ERISA plans
    - o   The educational credentials
    - o   Whether the person or entity is registered with the Securities and Exchange Commission under the Investment Advisors Act of 1940
    - o   An independent assessment of the person's or entity's qualifications by means of: (i) widely enjoyed reputation in the business of investments; (ii) client references; (iii) the advice of a professional third-party consultant.
    - o   The record of past performance with investments of the type contemplated

---

77   DOL Interpretive Bulletin 94-1.

- Ascertain the reasonableness of fees
- Review documents reflecting the relationship to be established
- Ensure adequate, periodic accountings and monitoring in the future

Thus, fiduciaries of any plan, including 401(k) plans, that seek to delegate investment responsibilities to independent investment advisors should follow the framework just given or a comparable one to ensure that their decisions to hire and continue with such a manager are prudent from the standpoint of ERISA. In other words, it is not enough to blindly hire an asset manager to manage all or a portion of the assets in the plan; rather, the plan fiduciary must undergo a fairly rigorous process in order to justify that the decision to hire any given manager was prudent in light of the circumstances surrounding that decision.

## The Diversification Rule

Generally, the investment diversification requirement of ERISA section 404(a)(1)(C) places an affirmative duty on a plan fiduciary to diversify plan investments unless, under the circumstances, it is clearly prudent not to diversify.

Under ERISA section 404(a)(2), an "eligible individual account plan" may acquire and hold qualifying employer securities or qualifying employer real property without regard to the diversification requirements or the diversification element of the prudent man rule. Profit sharing, stock bonus, thrift, or savings plans may qualify as eligible individual account plans as may certain money purchase pension plans.

# PLAN FEES AND EXPENSES

Recently, the DOL has focused increasing attention and audit enforcement activities on assessing whether 401(k) plans are properly allocating plan expenses. In response to the questions that arose during these audits, the DOL issued guidance.

The plan fiduciary is responsible for understanding and monitoring the fees and expenses charged against the assets of the plan. If a fee or expense is charged to the plan, the fiduciary must insure that such charge is: (1) a plan expense, (2) reasonable, and (3) properly allocated.[78] Moreover, such fees must be disclosed in the plan's summary plan description.

---

78 Department of Labor, Understanding Retirement Plan Fees and Expenses (May 2004).

## Permissible Plan Expense

Plan expenses are distinguished from settlor expenses because plan expenses relate solely to the management or administration of the plan. In traditional trust law parlance, a settlor is the party who designs, establishes, and funds a trust, while the fiduciary administers the trust in accordance with the terms adopted by the settlor. DOL has adopted this terminology for ERISA plans. Thus, an employer setting the terms of its employee benefit plan is a settlor, but when the employer administers the plan, it is a fiduciary.

The following list of fees and expenses may be charged to a 401(k) plan:[79]

- Accountant fees
- Actuarial fees
- Appraisal fees
- Annual valuations of trust assets
- Independent appraisal of employer stock in plan
- Attorney fees
- Investment advisory and management fees
- Third-party administrator fees
- Trustee and/or custodian fees
- Required bonding
- QDRO and QMCSO determination
- Claim processing and payment
- Check writing
- Distribution processing
- Hardship
- Calculating of benefit
- Reporting and disclosure
- Costs of amending plan for a required regulatory change
- Costs of implementing a plan termination
- Determination letter expenses for initial qualification of plan

---

79    Department of Labor, A Look at 401(k) Plan Fees for Employees (2004).

On the other hand, the following list of fees and expenses may not be charged to a 401(k) plan and thus are the responsibility of the employer (these are also known as settlor expenses):

- Plan design and implementation of plan costs
- Legal costs for corporate issues involved in establishing a plan
- Amending a plan for a business reason (and not a regulatory required amendment)
- Employer decisions regarding amending the plan, for example for an allocation or benefit formula change
- Plan termination costs other than those due to the implementation of the termination
- Costs associated with bringing the plan back into compliance under EPCRS
- Excise taxes and cost of preparation of the Form 5330 to pay the excise taxes

## Reasonableness of Fee or Expense

While ERISA does not set a specific level of fees, it does require that fees charged to a plan be "reasonable." The plan fiduciary is, therefore, responsible for determining whether an expense is reasonable and held to a high standard of care and diligence and must discharge their duties solely in the interest of the plan participants and their beneficiaries. Among other things, this means that employers must ensure that fees paid to service providers and other expenses of the plan are reasonable in light of the level and quality of services provided. In general, the fiduciary must consider if paying the expense is prudent and the expense is in the sole interest of the plan's participants and beneficiaries. The fiduciary should be mindful of the importance of using prudent judgment in determining whether an expense is a reasonable one.

The plan fiduciary must make the following determinations before causing a plan to purchase goods or services with plan assets:[80]

- The plan document does not prohibit the payment of the expense
- The goods or services (and related expense) are related to the fiduciary's administration of the plan and not to settlor decisions
- The expenditure is a prudent one and the amount is reasonable

---

80  DOL Advisory Opinion 01-01A (2001).

- If the service provider is a party in interest, the services arrangement meets the conditions of an ERISA exemption
- If the services are provided by a plan fiduciary, the amount paid to the fiduciary from the plan is limited to the fiduciary's direct expenses

## Allocation Method

In 2003, the DOL surprised many practitioners by reversing its 1994 position on the allocation of QDRO fees. After reviewing ERISA, the DOL concluded "plan sponsors and fiduciaries have considerable discretion in determining, as a matter of plan design or a matter of plan administration, how plan expenses will be allocated among participants and beneficiaries."[81] There are two primary issues regarding the allocation of expenses that can properly be charged to a defined contribution plan. They are:[82]

- The allocation of expenses on a pro rata, rather than a per capita basis, and
- The extent to which plan expenses may properly be charged to an individual account, rather than the plan as a whole.

First, a pro rata allocation is based upon a proportional share of plan assets. For example, if participant A's account balance comprises 10 percent of all plan assets, his account would bear 10 percent of the expense allocation. In the alternative, a per capita allocation is allocated equally to each participant, regardless of account values.

The DOL stated that where the plan document specifically provides the allocation method to be used, fiduciaries must follow the prescribed method. Failure to do so would be an unauthorized alteration of plan benefits. Absent specific plan provisions, fiduciaries must follow a method that is prudent and solely in the interest of all participants. The method chosen must have a rational basis, with some reasonable relationship to the services provided or available to an individual account.

The DOL's language on this issue is actually quite general, and few concrete examples are given. A per capita allocation may be appropriate with certain fixed administrative expenses, such as record keeping, legal, auditing, annual reporting, or claims processing. Investment management fees would more likely qualify for the pro rata basis because the DOL's rationale is "with regard to services which provide investment advice to individual participants, a fiduciary

---

81    DOL Field Assistance Bulletin ("FAB") 2003-3, May 19, 2003.
82    Id.

may be able to justify the allocation of such expenses on either a pro rata or per capita basis and without regard to actual utilization of the services by particular individual accounts."[83] The guidelines for the proper allocation method appear to be broad and open to interpretation. Prudence and reasonableness should be the primary concerns.

Second, the DOL provides guidance on charging specific fees to a participant's account. Recent interpretations differ from the above discussion on allocating expenses among all participants. The DOL referring to its 1994 position on QDRO determination fees concluded that "neither the analyses [n]or conclusions set forth in that opinion are legally compelled by the language of the statute [ERISA]."[84] It noted that ERISA places few constraints on how expenses are allocated among participants, and therefore the same principles applicable to determining the method of allocating expenses among all participants should apply to permissible allocation of specific expenses to individuals rather than the plan as a whole.

On this subject, the DOL did provide specific examples of expenses, to the extent they are reasonable, which can be charged to an individual account.[85] They are as follows:

- Hardship withdrawals
- Calculation of benefits payable under various distribution options
- Qualifying a domestic relations order
- Benefit distributions, including periodic check writing expenses
- Administrative expenses of accounts of separated vested participants

Regarding the last item, the DOL stated that it would be reasonable for fiduciaries to charge administrative expenses against accounts of terminated participants even where the plan sponsor pays such expenses for active participants.

Initially, the IRS expressed concerns that only charging the former participants and beneficiaries for expenses could lead to a significant detriment.[86] The IRS concluded in 2004 that fees imposed on the former plan participants and beneficiaries would be analogous to fess charged in the marketplace had the assets be held in an IRA.

---

83    DOL Field Assistance Bulletin ("FAB") 2003-3, May 19, 2003.
84    Advisory Opinion No. 2001-01A.
85    DOL Field Assistance Bulletin 2003-3 (2003).
86    IRS Rev. Rul. 96-47.

## Obligations Regarding "Float"

Service providers to 401(k) plans often receive some investment earnings on funds in transit. "Float" is the short-term interest earned on such funds. The DOL's long-standing position is that any float earned on plan assets is considered part of the plan's earnings. Service providers may retain the float as part of their compensation; however, they must fully disclose the arrangement to the plan sponsor. Moreover, as a fee of the plan, to satisfy ERISA's fiduciary standards, plan fiduciaries must: (1) review service providers and arrangements for the treatment of float, (2) determine how the float is generated, and (3) evaluate the role and amount of float in the overall compensation to the provider.[87]

# FIDUCIARY RESPONSIBILITY IN PARTICIPANT-DIRECTED 401(k) PLANS

The fiduciary responsibility rules take on special application in 401(k) plans that allow for participant-directed investments. In those instances, the plan fiduciaries are transferring the investment allocation responsibility to employees and may receive in exchange a consequent reduction in their own level of personal liability.

For several years, the DOL had struggled to finalize the section 404(c) regulations that govern the transfer of investment control to participants. The final regulations were issued on October 13, 1992. In essence, section 404(c) of ERISA relieves plan fiduciaries of liability for investment losses if the plan permits its participants to exercise control over the investments and the losses resulted from the participant's exercise of control. This section of ERISA offers a compelling story to plan sponsors, and this story has largely fueled the movement toward participant-directed plans.

Compliance with the requirements of section 404(c) is optional. Plans that elect not to comply with the requirements do not violate ERISA solely due to that election. However, an election not to be treated as a section 404(c) plan means that the plan fiduciaries may continue to be held responsible under ERISA for the results of participants' investments. For this reason, compliance with the regulation is advised.

Finally, it should be recognized that plan fiduciaries that seek the protections of section 404(c) would always have the burden of proof in litigation that they complied with the regulation.

---

87    DOL Field Assistance Bulletin ("FAB") 2002-3, November 5, 2002.

## Residual Fiduciary Responsibilities

Sponsors should be cognizant of the fact that section 404(c) is an exception to a larger rule and alleviates the plan fiduciaries only from potential liability for investment losses resulting from participants' exercise of control over their own accounts; it does not provide categorical relief from all of ERISA's fiduciary responsibility provisions.

Rather, section 404(c) insulates plan fiduciaries from the results of individual participants' own investment allocation decisions. Thus, before a plan fiduciary can ever hope to be protected under section 404(c), ERISA's general prudence requirements must be satisfied with respect to all of the following:

- The actual prudent and diverse selection of investment vehicle
- The periodic performance review of these investment vehicles
- The ongoing due diligence determination that the alternatives remain suitable investment vehicles for plan participants

Only after having completed this process are plan fiduciaries in a position to take the final step, under section 404(c), to move the control of investments into the hands of participants under the procedures specified in the regulations. Most importantly, a plan fiduciary who merely transfers to participants the control over investments, ignoring his or her nondelegable fiduciary responsibilities as just outlined, fails to gain any protections under section 404(c) and may actually increase his or her potential liability under ERISA.[88]

# THE FOUR HURDLES TO MANAGING FIDUCIARY RESPONSIBILITY IN PARTICIPANT-DIRECTED 401(K) PLANS

## Hurdle 1: Prudent Selection of Investment Fund or Advisor

Fiduciaries of participant-directed 401(k) plans have a special relationship to participants. Because they are essentially preselecting the investment options that will in turn be provided to plan participants, they are engaging in a

---

88  DOL Reg 2550.404c-1. See also, Perdue, "ERISA Liability of Fiduciaries and Plan Service Providers Is a Growing Concern," 2JTEB 19 (May/Jun 1994), and Jenkins, "Fiduciaries of Participant-Directed Accounts Must Plan to Protect Themselves," 2JTEB 116 (Sept/Oct 1994).

substantial fiduciary function. The exercise of this function requires plan fiduciaries to act prudently in their selection of these different investment options.

In making this prudent selection, plan fiduciaries need to follow the same fiduciary prudence guidelines outlined earlier. As a practical matter, plan fiduciaries need to take an active role in selecting investment managers for each category in the plan, applying the standards of prudence as well as the exclusive benefit requirement. The selection of each investment manager should be made after exhaustive due diligence and a determination that the manager is the most appropriate of all those surveyed.

Again, because of the relative immaturity of 401(k) plans in the scheme of fiduciary responsibility law, it is too soon to look to the courts for the direct establishment of standards to be used in selecting the particular investment options in a self-directed plan. The DOL has indicated, however, that the standard to be applied is nothing more than an extension of the standard applied in ordinary employer-directed plans.

The DOL emphasizes that the act of designating investment alternatives in an ERISA section 404(c) plan is a fiduciary function to which the limitation on liability provided by section 404(c) is not applicable. All of the fiduciary provisions of ERISA remain applicable to both the initial designation of investment alternatives and investment managers and the ongoing determination that such alternatives and managers remain suitable and prudent investment alternatives for the plan.[89] Therefore, the particular plan fiduciaries responsible for performing these functions must do so in accordance with ERISA.

Therefore, in selecting the investment fund or manager, plan fiduciaries should consider carefully their conduct in investigating, evaluating and making the hiring decision. The process in which a fiduciary engages in making this decision is the central inquiry in determining whether a fiduciary fulfilled his or her responsibilities in selecting the investments for plan participants. In litigation, plan fiduciaries will be required to prove that they engaged in a thoughtfully and prudent selection process. Therefore, it is essential that the plan's decision-making process be thoroughly documented. Additionally, an investment policy statement should describe the process and criteria for the decisions.

Considering the substantial risk of litigation, plan fiduciaries should further bear in mind that they have an affirmative obligation under ERISA to seek independent advice from a qualified professional when they lack the requisite education, experience, and skill. Once again, in litigation, the plan fiduciary would be required to prove that he or she either (1) possessed the requisite expertise or (2) received independent advice from a qualified professional.

---

89    DOL's regulations under ERISA section 404(c).

Thus, the following might serve as a general guideline for plan fiduciaries in their selection of investments to be offered to participants as investment selections in the plan:

- Use the advice of a professional third-party advisor or consultant to review competitors and to define asset categories
- Establish competitive bidding procedure; no organization should be preselected or precluded (except for parties-in-interest)
- Request written proposals from all bidding organizations
- Review the competitors for any party-in-interest relationship
- Evaluate the organization's qualifications, from the 401(k) asset management standpoint, including all the considerations noted earlier
- Ascertain the reasonableness of fees relative to proposed services by establishing a grid comparison
- Ensure adequate, periodic monitoring in the future

## The Use of a Financial Advisor or Consulting Organization

The use of third-party financial advisors or consultants to assist the 401(k) plan fiduciary in the selection of investment management organizations is simply an extension of what has long been the practice of prudent plan fiduciaries. This practice is gaining prominence in the 401(k) area, in view of the substantial responsibility in selecting investment options for participants.

As a practical matter, the 401(k) plan fiduciary is entitled to rely on the information, data statistics, or analyses provided by the financial advisor or consulting organization in exercising his or her fiduciary duties, provided that the fiduciary exercises prudence in selecting, monitoring, and retaining the advisor or consultant. Generally, the plan fiduciary will be deemed to have acted prudently in the selection and retention of the advisors or consultant if he or she has no reason to doubt the competence, integrity, or responsibility of such persons or organizations.

## Choosing a 401(k) Provider for the Wrong Reasons

Although there is always a powerful consideration of administrative convenience and simplicity, plan fiduciaries must be careful not to select a 401(k) provider to handle all aspects of the plan investments solely for the reason of administrative convenience. Although this is certainly an important consideration, convenience is not a valid reason in and of itself from the standpoint of ERISA.

Plan fiduciaries must keep in mind the exclusive purpose rule of ERISA, which directs a fiduciary to act solely in the interest of participants and beneficiaries and for the exclusive purpose of providing benefits to participants. It is questionable, to say the least, whether the selection of an organization because of administrative convenience or the attainment of a corporate line of credit, rather than on the merits of that organization's investment expertise in all relevant asset categories, is a prudent decision for the exclusive benefit of participants. Rather, the decision to hire a particular investment manager should be based on an objective evaluation of the standards mentioned earlier.

### Select Experts in Each Asset Category

As discussed later in this chapter, participant-directed plans need to offer participants a minimum selection of investment options among various investment categories. In the discussion of those categories, it is important to note that from the standpoint of fiduciary responsibility that the company selected to manage the participants' assets have breadth of experience in all relevant asset classes. A few 401(k) providers today have such breadth; others have teamed up to create unbundled multi-fund products. Still, certain of these multi-fund products still have administrative shortcomings as described in Chapter 6.

## Hurdle 2: Participants Must Be In "Control" Over Their Investments

In essence, ERISA section 404(c) attempts to immunize plan fiduciaries from any liability resulting from participants' control over investment allocation decisions. Any protections provided under section 404(c) exist under the theory that a plan fiduciary should not be responsible for that which a participant is in control of. Thus, the primary inquiry under section 404(c) focuses on whether the participants are in control of their investments.

This is reflected in the DOL's core requirements for section 404(c) compliance:

- The plan must provide the participant with the opportunity to exercise control over the assets in his or her account.

- The participant must in fact exercise independent control with respect to the investment of these assets.[90]

---

90   See 29 C.F.R. §2550.404c-1(b)(1).

## Requirement One: Opportunity to Exercise Control

There are a number of practical requirements set forth under the regulations to ensure that participants are given the opportunity to exercise control over the investments.

### Broad Range Requirement

The DOL has consistently adhered to the view that a participant only has an opportunity to exercise control if he or she is offered a broad range of investment alternatives. The definition of broad range requires that the plan offer to its participants the opportunity to direct their investments into three different investment categories. Each of these three categories must have "material different risk and return characteristics."[91] Taken together, these three investment categories must permit participants to construct an appropriate investment mix with appropriate corresponding risk and return characteristics. Each investment alternative must also be of a type that, when combined with the other investment alternatives, tends to minimize through diversification the overall risk of a participant's portfolio.

Some commentators have argued that these broad range requirements are vague and therefore difficult to apply.[92] Yet, the final regulation of the DOL is intended to give plan sponsors broad latitude in developing combinations of investment alternatives that meet the broad range requirement. Because the determination of what constitutes a broad range requires considerable expertise, plan sponsors are strongly urged to rely on the advice of a qualified investment management consultant.

### Diversification Requirement

In order for the categories to be deemed a broad range of alternatives, each investment alternative must be diversified in and of itself so that participants are given the opportunity to minimize the risk of large losses. For this reason, employer securities cannot be used as one of the core investment alternatives intended to satisfy the broad range requirements of the regulation. Employer securities would not themselves represent a diversified investment alternative.

In order to accomplish the diversification requirement, the regulations permit the plan to offer so-called look-through investment vehicles. These consist of mutual funds, bank collective funds, insurance company pooled separate accounts, GICs, or a separately managed account for the plan. In essence, these

---

91  Id.
92  See Don Carlson and Timothy Goodman, Are you Protected? Demonstrating Compliance with Section 404(c) of ERISA, Employee Benefits Update (February 12, 2004).

look-through investment vehicles permit employees to achieve instant diversification in any given asset category.

ERISA's legislative history offers guidance on the diversification requirement. A prudent fiduciary must consider the facts and circumstances of each case. The factors to consider include: (1) the purpose of the plan; (2) the amount of plan assets; (3) financial and industrial conditions; (4) the type of investment; (5) distribution based on geographic location; (6) distribution based on industries; (7) the dates of maturity.[93] Against a claim of failure to diversify, the fiduciary must demonstrate that it was clearly prudent not to diversify.

### Frequency of Opportunity to Give Investment Instructions

To exercise control, participants must be able to change their investment allocations with some frequency. The regulations have created a relatively complex set of standards governing the required frequency for investment changes in different instances.

The general rule provides that the opportunity to exercise control will not exist unless participants are given the opportunity to give investment instructions with a frequency that is appropriate in light of the volatility to which the investment may reasonably be expected to be subject. This principle is known as the "general volatility rule."[94] However, regardless of the frequency required under the general volatility rule, with regard to the three core investment vehicles constituting the broad range, investment changes must be permitted once every three months. This is known in the regulation as the "three-month minimum."[95]

Although there is no restriction on a plan's ability to offer other investment alternatives in addition to the three core alternatives, it should be noted that there would be no section 404(c) relief to plan fiduciaries with respect to amounts invested in investment alternatives that do not permit investment instructions with a frequency commensurate with the reasonably expected volatility of the investment alternative.

---

93    House Report to ERISA, H. Rep. No. 93-1280; 93rd Cong., 2nd Sess. See Donovan v. Guaranty National Bank, 4 Emp. Benefits Cas. (BNA) 1686 (S.D. W. Va. 1983).

94    Under ERISA section 404(c) plan must at a minimum provide a participant or beneficiary an opportunity to give investment instructions at least once within any three-month period (referred to elsewhere herein as the "three-month minimum"). Paragraph (b)(2)(ii)(C)(1) of the final regulation clarifies that the minimum of three core alternatives subject to the three-month minimum must itself constitute a broad range of investment alternatives.

95    ERISA §404(c).

This rule provides a difficult standard for plan sponsors in view of the fact that no examples are provided in the regulation demonstrating the types of investments that would require investment changes more frequently than once every three months. Moreover, the DOL has imposed an ongoing obligation on the part of plan fiduciaries to review the volatility of all investment selections.

Fiduciaries of an ERISA section 404(c) plan should periodically review the volatility of its investment alternatives to ensure that the transfer frequency permitted with respect to each alternative continues to be appropriate.

As a result, plan sponsors are well advised to: (1) determine the appropriate transfer frequency given the expected volatility of the investments, and (2) monitor the volatility of the investment alternatives to ensure that the transfer frequency continues to be appropriate.

## The Volatile Investment Transferability Rule

In those instances where a plan permits participants to invest in additional noncore investment alternatives in which investment transfers are allowed more frequently than once every three months, the regulation imposes additional complex rules governing the transfer frequency. This rule, called the volatile investment transferability rule, is necessary because the ability to transfer assets to or from a volatile investment has meaning only where there is in fact another investment vehicle available that can just as readily transfer out or accept assets. In essence, this rule requires that participants be given the opportunity to direct their investment alternatives with a frequency commensurate with the volatility of the more volatile investment vehicle.

Under the regulation, there are two methods for accommodating transfers between core and noncore investments. Under the first method, at least one of the core investment alternatives must permit participants to give investment instructions as frequently as they are permitted to give investment instructions with respect to any additional non–core investment alternative made available by the plan. In addition, the core investment alternative selected to satisfy this requirement need only permit such instructions with regard to transfers into the core alternative.

Rather than permitting transfers directly into core alternatives, the regulation also permits the plan to allow participants to direct the transfer from the more volatile investment into a temporary holding account until such time as they may, under the terms of the plan, further direct the assets into at least one of the three core investment alternatives.

## Special Transfer Rules for Employer Stock

In general, the methods for accommodating transfers from employer securities are essentially the same as for all other alternatives except that participants must be given the ability to direct their investments from employer securities into any of the available core investment alternatives.[96] In short, all of the core investment alternatives must permit participants to give investment instructions with regard to transfers into each of the alternatives as frequently as they are permitted to give investment instructions with respect to employer securities.

### Disclosure to Be Made To Participants

In addition to the above requirements, the regulation requires that participants receive sufficient information so that they are able to make informed investment decisions. The regulation requires that certain information be furnished to all participants and that certain other information be furnished when requested.

The requirements listed here should form the skeleton of any participant communication program. As such, these requirements are the minimum of what must be provided to participants so that they are able to make informed investment decisions. Sponsors should work with their plan providers to flush out these minimum standards in an effort to provide sufficient information given the particular characteristics of their plan, company, and employee base.

The following information is required to be furnished to all participants:[97]

- An explanation that the plan is intended to constitute a section 404(c) plan and that plan fiduciaries may be relieved of liability for losses that are the result of participants' investment instructions

- A description of the investment alternatives in the plan, including a general description of the investment objectives and risk and return characteristics of each

- Identification of any designated investment managers

- An explanation of how to give investment instructions, any limits or restrictions on giving instructions, and any limits on the exercise of voting, tender, or similar rights

- A description of any transaction fees or expenses that are charged to the participant's account

- A description of the information available on request and the identity of the person or persons responsible for providing the information

- Immediately following an investment in an investment alternative subject to the Securities Act of 1933, a copy of the most recent prospectus, unless the prospectus was furnished immediately before the participant's investment

---

96    Preamble to ERISA §404(c).
97    DOL Reg. §2550.404c-1(b)(2)(B)(1).

- Subsequent to an investment, materials provided to the plan relative to the exercise of voting, tender, or similar rights, to the extent such rights are passed through to participants

The following information must be provided on request to participants:[98]

- A description of the annual operating expenses borne by investment alternatives, such as the investment management fees
- Copies of any prospectuses, financial statements, and reports furnished to the plan relating to the investment alternatives
- A listing of the assets comprising the portfolio of an investment alternative that holds plan assets; the value of such assets; and, in the case of fixed rate contracts of banks or insurance companies, the name of the issuers of the contract, the terms of the contract, and the rate of return of the contract
- Information concerning the value of shares or units of investment alternatives available to participants, as well as information concerning the past and current investment performance of the alternative
- Information concerning the value of shares or units in investment alternatives held in the account of the participant

These standards are rigorous and probably require more disclosure than any other regulation designed to protect the interest of an investor (participant). Interestingly, these standards provide only the starting point for fiduciaries of participant-directed plans. Plan fiduciaries still must work with their plan providers to be certain that these required disclosures (and other information) are communicated in a way that all participants are able to fully understand the plan. Plan fiduciaries that approach these as boilerplate, fine print disclosures will continue to be susceptible to liability.

## Requirement Two: Actual Exercise of Independent Control

The entire regulatory structure of ERISA section 404(c) hinges on whether a participant is in fact in control over his or her investments. When it can be shown that the participant in fact exercised control over the assets in his or her account, the plan fiduciary will be insulated from the results of a participant's investment control. The corollary to this rule is also true: when it can be shown that a participant was not in fact in control over his or her investments, the plan fiduciary can be held liable for the results of the participant's investment decisions.

---

98   Id.

The regulations maintain that whether a participant has indeed exercised such independent control is to be determined on a case-by-case basis.[99] This is problematic because there is no real guidance in the regulations in making this determination, and it is the fiduciary's obligation to prove that any given investment decision was in fact controlled by the participant.

Under the regulation, a participant will not be considered to have exercised control over the assets in his or her account unless the participant has provided affirmative investment instructions with respect to such assets.[100] In other words, plan fiduciaries will not be relieved of responsibility for investment decisions under section 404(c) unless participants who have exercised independent control have affirmatively made those decisions. Thus, when participants fail to give investment instructions, the common practice of placing the participant's assets in a so-called safe investment will not provide any relief to plan fiduciaries. As in other non-404(c)-type plans, fiduciaries of ERISA section 404(c) plans have a duty to provide for the investment of idle plan assets, and lack of participant direction will not absolve a fiduciary of such duties. In short, until an affirmative instruction is received, there can be no relief under section 404(c) of ERISA.

However, where a participant is afforded the opportunity to exercise voting, tender, or similar rights and is provided the information necessary to exercise such rights, the regulation provides that a participant will be considered to have exercised control with respect to such rights even if the participant takes no action.

In addition, a participant does not in fact exercise control if the plan fiduciary fails to reveal facts that would bear on the suitability of the transaction from the participant's standpoint, unless disclosing these facts would violate securities or banking laws.

Moreover, a participant is not in control when he or she has been subjected to "improper influence."[101] Thus, plan fiduciaries should not render any advice to participants. Rather, fiduciaries should rely on the consultants to the plan to provide advice to participants.

Finally, if the fiduciary knows that a participant is legally incompetent, he or she must disregard that participant's investment instructions.

---

99    See DOL Reg. §2550.404c-1.

100    Id.

101    DOL Reg. §2550.404c-1(c)(2).

# Hurdle 3: Monitoring the Investment Managers

As noted earlier, the actual selection by the plan fiduciary of an investment manager is itself a fiduciary decision subject to the prudent man standard and other ERISA safeguards. Thus, if the plan fiduciary considers hiring the manager or managers, the fiduciary cannot be held liable for this decision unless it can be shown that the hiring decision was somehow imprudent or unreasonable.

However, the duty of the plan fiduciary in a 401(k) plan does not end with the appointment of investment managers. The DOL has set forth the following general ongoing responsibilities:[102]

- At reasonable intervals the performance of trustees and other fiduciaries should be reviewed by the appointing fiduciary in such manner as may be reasonably expected to ensure that their performance has been in compliance with the terms of the plan and statutory standards, and satisfies the needs of the plan. No single procedure will be appropriate in all cases; the procedure adopted may vary in accordance with the nature of the plan and other facts and circumstances relative to the choice of the procedure.

- Although this requirement applies universally to all plans, regardless of type, the DOL has specifically extended the requirement to the participant-directed plans.

- The plan fiduciary has a fiduciary obligation to periodically evaluate the performance of such vehicles to determine, based on that evaluation, whether the vehicles should continue to be available as participant investment options.

In addition, as noted earlier, the DOL has created a new obligation for plan fiduciaries of participant-directed plans to review the volatility of the plan's investment alternatives to ensure that the transfer frequency permitted with respect to each alternative continues to be appropriate.

From these statements and from court rulings, it is clear that the plan fiduciary must take certain actions in order to discharge his or her obligation to monitor the performance and volatility of the asset manager or managers. The following standard is recommended as an appropriate method for monitoring performance.

- Require the trustee or investment manager to prepare periodic reports about the specific investments of the plan assets under the manager's control, including investment performance and volatility.

---

102  29 C.F.R. § 2509.75-8 at FR-17.

- Compare actual investments and investment performance to the goals of the plan as communicated to the asset manager and to the investment guidelines set forth in the investment management agreement.

- Review investment performance and volatility of common indexes or other similarly investment portfolios for comparison to the investment results of the investment manager.

- Obtain an evaluation by an independent entity experienced in evaluating investment performance of the investments and investment performance and volatility versus relevant benchmark indexes.

## Hurdle 4: Ongoing Due Diligence

As a final matter, to manage fiduciary responsibility in a participant-directed plan, the plan fiduciary must exercise ongoing due diligence over the investments and the investment managers. In this regard, the DOL has stated that the ongoing duty to consider the suitability of a designated investment vehicle encompasses a continuing determination that the vehicle remains a prudent investment option.[103]

# SECTION 404(C) PROTECTION

One of the common themes throughout this chapter is the notion that ERISA section 404(c) does not relieve plan fiduciaries from all of their fiduciary obligations under the plan. As noted earlier, plan fiduciaries are still required to perform all of their nondelegable fiduciary obligations under the plan such as prudent selection, ongoing monitoring, and due diligence. These obligations are in fact identical to the general obligations imposed on a fiduciary in an employer-directed plan. This raises the question whether in fact maintaining a participant-directed plan offers any real advantage to plan fiduciaries in terms of reducing their potential exposure.

Compliance with 404(c) is unlikely to significantly decrease the incidence of lawsuits alleging fiduciary misconduct when a participant-directed investment goes sour. The proposed regulation's requirement that section 404(c) relief will be unavailable if the fiduciary has not disseminated sufficient information to participants to allow them to render prudent investment decisions affords participants and the DOL and effective enforcement tool by which to continue to impose liability on plan fiduciaries for imprudent investments.

---

103  Preamble to DOL 404(c) Regulations, 57 Fed. Reg. 46906,46922.

Rather than assert that a fiduciary has authorized a substantively imprudent investment, participants will simply argue that they did not receive enough information to render a prudent investment decision.

Given the scope of disclosures required under the regulation, and the fact that plan fiduciaries retain all of their prior responsibilities under ERISA, it appears unlikely that merely maintaining a participant-directed plan actually reduces a plan fiduciary's potential liability. Nevertheless, to the extent that a plan allows participants to direct their own investments, the prudent plan fiduciaries should do the following:

- Continue to perform all of their basic responsibilities
- Comply with the regulations
- Make every attempt to communicate information in a straightforward and sufficient manner

# FIDUCIARY LIABILITY UNDER ERISA

In addition to ERISA's strict parameters on fiduciary conduct, the act further permits legal action to be brought by a participant, beneficiary, or other fiduciary against a plan fiduciary for a breach of duty. In those cases where the fiduciary is found to in fact have violated these duties, the fiduciary may be found to be personally liable for any losses to the plan resulting from the breach of duty, and any profits earned by the fiduciary through the illegal use of plan assets must be turned over to the plan. ERISA also gives the court the power to order other appropriate relief such as the removal of the fiduciary.

However, a fiduciary may not be held responsible for any breaches of fiduciary duty that occurred before the time he or she became a fiduciary or after the time he or she ceased to be a fiduciary.

All fiduciaries should be mindful of the principle of ongoing fiduciary breach, which holds that even through a fiduciary may not be personally liable or responsible for the original breach, if he or she knows of the breach, that fiduciary is required to take measures to remedy the situation. The failure to take remedial steps might constitute an independent breach of fiduciary duty in and of itself.

## Determination of Losses to the Plan

A disturbing trend in fiduciary responsibility cases is the tendency of some courts to define broadly the word loss, which means that plan fiduciaries may find themselves liable for violations that at first glance do not appear to have resulted in an apparent economic loss to plan assets.

Consider the following examples as illustrations about how some courts have defined loss where the fiduciary was held to have violated his fiduciary duties

1. A plan actually experienced a healthy and positive return in an investment that violated ERISA, but the court compared that return to the return that would have been realized if the funds had been invested in an alternative, proper investment over the same period of time. When several alternatives were equally plausible, the court assumed that the funds would have been invested in the most profitable investment and required the fiduciary to make up the difference

2. The investment manager failed to follow investment policy that limited equity investment to 50 percent of the portfolio, and the plan nevertheless earned a healthy return on those equity investments, but the court held the investment manager liable for the amount the plan could have earned had the assets not been improperly invested.

3. The court found a violation of fiduciary duty when the investment manager invested 70 percent of the assets of a profit-sharing plan in thirty-year treasury bonds. Because of required distributions, the investment manager was forced to sell some bonds at a loss. The court faulted the manager for failing to know the cash-flow requirements of the plan. As a result, the court ordered the manager to pay the plan the difference between what it would have earned had it been funded with bonds containing staggered maturity dates and what it actually earned.

4. The court ordered an investment manager found in fiduciary violation to pay the difference between the plan's actual earnings and what the plan would have earned during the relevant period, as measured by the Standard and Poor's 500 Index.

## Return of Profits and/or Equitable Relief

In addition to having to recoup "losses" to the plan under fiduciary liability theory, a violating fiduciary is always required to return to the plan any profits realized through the abuse of his or her position or trust. Moreover, equitable relief for a breach of fiduciary duty is authorized under section 409 of ERISA even if there are no losses to the plan and no disgorged profits.

The following are examples of the types of equitable relief fashioned by some courts:

- Removal of trustee of fiduciary

- Rescission of employment agreement and order to pay back all salary paid

- Prejudgment interest
- Postjudgment interest

## Civil Penalties

In addition to possible liability to the plan or to participants for breaches of fiduciary obligation, the DOL may impose a 20 percent civil penalty under section 502 of ERISA. This penalty is at the discretion of the DOL, which may seek to impose this penalty by court order or by direct settlement with the violating fiduciaries. In some instances, the DOL may choose to reduce or waive the penalty if the fiduciary acted in good faith or will not be able to restore the plan losses without severe financial hardship. The penalty may be avoided by participating in the DOL's Voluntary Fiduciary Compliance (VFC) Program. The VFC Program allows fiduciaries to voluntarily correct breaches and prohibited transactions and thereby avoids civil action and penalties. The program is available to a plan not currently under investigation by the DOL.

Examples of situations where a fiduciary may breach ERISA duties include the following.

1. **Failure to prudently select**
   When a plan fiduciary or committee fails to properly select the investment managers for the 401(k) plan, the participants might seek to recover the difference between what they actually earned and what they might have earned had an appropriate selection been made.

2. **Failure to provide for actual participant control**
   When a plan fiduciary of a participant-directed plan fails to provide participants with the requisite broad selection of investments or fails to allow participants the ability to make changes frequently enough, the fiduciary could be held liable for participants' individual investment allocation decisions. If those decisions were overly aggressive or ultra-conservative, the plan fiduciary could be required to make up the difference between what the participant could have earned had he or she been properly invested and what he or she actually earned.

3. **Failure to provide sufficient investment information**
   In a participant-directed plan, if plan fiduciaries fail to provide sufficient information so that participants can make intelligent and informed long-term investment allocation decisions, plan fiduciaries could be held liable and responsible for the allocation by any participant who failed to understand the nature of his or her decisions. Again, the fiduciaries could be held liable for the difference between what the participant might have

earned had he or she been properly invested and what he or she actually did earn.

4. **Mislabeling of investments**

   In a participant-directed plan, the plan fiduciary communicated that one of the investment vehicles was guaranteed and could not lose principal. In fact, the issuer of that instrument is unable to pay in full the principal value of the investment or the accrued interest. In this event, the plan fiduciaries could be held liable and required to make up the difference to participants under the theory that they imprudently selected the investment and they imprudently represented that investment to participants as guaranteed.

5. **Failure to monitor**

   In a participant-directed plan, if the plan fiduciaries fail to monitor the performance on a periodic basis and that performance over time is found to be deficient in comparison to benchmark indexes, the fiduciary might be charged to make up the difference between actual performance and the benchmark index performance under the theory that the fiduciary failed to monitor the investments and to take corrective action.

6. **Failure to monitor volatility**

   In a participant-directed plan, if the plan fiduciaries fail to monitor the volatility of the investment alternatives and it is found later that the volatility of one or more of the investment alternatives necessitated greater transfer frequency, the plan could lose all protections under section 404(c) and the fiduciaries could be responsible for participants' investment decisions.

7. **Failure to perform due diligence**

   In a participant-directed 401(k) plan, if the sponsor performed no due diligence review over the investment advisors managing the assets in the plan and one of those advisors experienced extensive turnover of portfolio managers, which later results in a performance decline, the plan fiduciaries might be held liable to make up the difference to the plan under the theory that the advisor failed to perform due diligence on an ongoing basis with respect to the plan's asset managers.

## Co-fiduciary Liability

In addition to liability for a fiduciary's own breaches, a fiduciary may also be held liable for the breaches committed by other co-fiduciaries if the first fiduciary does any of the following:

- Knowingly participates in or undertakes to conceal a co-fiduciary's breach, aware that such act or omission is a breach
- Fails to meet his or her own responsibilities and, as a result, enables another to breach a fiduciary obligation through neglect of duties, enabling the other fiduciary to commit a breach
- Becomes aware of another fiduciary's breach and makes no reasonable efforts under the circumstances to remedy the breach

Plan fiduciaries always should attempt to remedy any breach by other plan fiduciaries. When a plan fiduciary believes that a co-fiduciary has committed a breach, resignation by the fiduciary as a protest against such a breach is not generally considered sufficient to discharge the fiduciary's affirmative duty under section 405(a)(3), which requires the fiduciary to make reasonable efforts under the circumstances to remedy the breach.

Possible ways to remedy the breach might include disposal of an asset, notification to the sponsoring organization, instigation of a lawsuit against the co-fiduciary, or notification of the breach to the DOL.

## Liability Related to Employer Stock Investments

The emergence of recent lawsuits where participants are claiming fiduciary breach for the investment for plan assets in employer stock raises awareness of fiduciary duties. The claims, which remain in the trail stage as of this publication, fall in the following two categories:

- The fiduciaries breached their duty of loyalty by failing to disclose pertinent information to the participants
- The fiduciaries breached their duty of prudence by not diversifying assets invested in company stock

# MANAGING FIDUCIARY RESPONSIBILITY

Managing fiduciary responsibility is no easy task. However, there are many resources available, including financial advisors, attorneys, and consultants. In attempts to better manage fiduciary responsibility, employers should engage the appropriate resources and follow these steps:

- Maintain an updated plan document and SPD
- Appoint and monitor qualified plan fiduciaries

- Conduct an annual retirement plan meeting to review plan investments, expenses, and operations
- Collect and review the information
- Document decisions
- Maintain an investment policy statement
- Offer participants a well-diversified menu of prudently selected investment options
- Comply with ERISA section 404(c) if the plan is a participant directed plan
- Ensure that participant deferrals and loan payments are deposited in a timely manner
- Conduct annual plan testing
- File annual reports with the governmental agencies
- Follow the provisions of the plan
- Act in the best interest of the plan and its participants

# THE TWO CATEGORIES OF PEOPLE UNDER ERISA

Under ERISA, there are two categories of people whose conduct or activities are subject to legal constraints and standards: plan fiduciaries and parties-in-interest.[104] Fiduciaries, as discussed later, are those people with some true influential power or discretion over the plan. This definition includes generally those people who have the authority and responsibility with respect to the management of the plan and its assets, regardless of their formal title. Such a person is considered to have such power over the plan to require the application of special fiduciary responsibility provisions.

Parties-in-interest, on the other hand, include people who have a close relationship to the plan or the sponsor but do not have discretion over the plan or its assets. Because of these people's close relationship to the plan, and the opportunity for abuse, any transaction with a party-in-interest must be reviewed to see whether it violates ERISA's prohibited transaction provisions. These prohibitions, along with the definition of party-in-interest, are discussed later in this chapter.

---

104  ERISA §3(14).

## Figure 7-2: Fiduciary Classifications

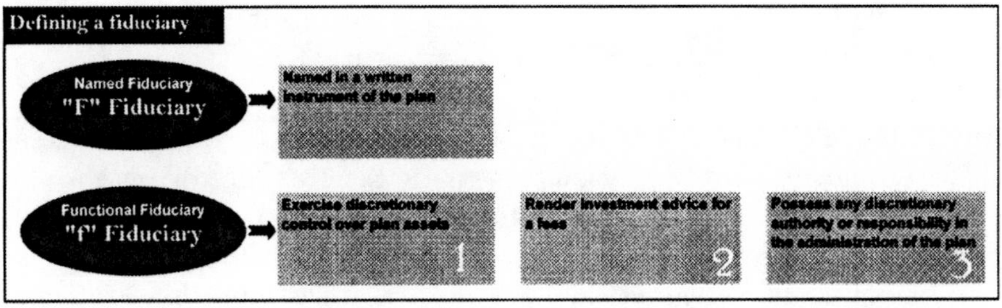

# WHO IS A FIDUCIARY?

As a practical matter, the issue about whether a person is a fiduciary of a plan only arises when someone is alleging a violation of some fiduciary responsibility. In the case of 401(k) plans, this issue might arise when there has been a loss of assets due to poor investment practices, failure to monitor investments, or failure to perform due diligence on the investment advisers to the plan. In any event, when such instances occur, participants may look to the fiduciary as a way to make themselves whole.

Any person who exercises discretion or authority with respect to the control or maintenance of employee benefit plan assets will be deemed a fiduciary under ERISA section 3(21). Therefore, the definition of fiduciary under ERISA includes any person who performs any of the following:[105]

- Is named in the plan document as a fiduciary or as appointed as a fiduciary in accordance with a procedure in the plan document

- Exercises any discretionary authority or control over the management of the plan generally or with respect to the management or disposition of plan assets

- Renders investment advice with respect to plan assets for a fee or other compensation

- Exercises any discretionary authority or responsibility in the plan's administration

The first category is a named fiduciary or in analogous terms to the SEC's insider trading terms of a capital *I* insider, a capital *F* fiduciary. A named fiduciary

---

105  ERISA §3(21)(A).

is the fiduciary pursuant to ERISA's requirement that a plan's written instrument, or document, actually name a fiduciary. The named fiduciary can be an individual, a group of individuals, the employer or company, or a third-party company. The sponsoring employer and trustee are always named fiduciaries.

The next categories are considered functional fiduciaries or in analogous terms to the SEC's insider trading terms of a lowercase *i* insider, a lowercase *f* fiduciary. A functional fiduciary is a person who exercises control over the plan or its investments, or gives investment advice, but who was not formally appointed to perform those roles.

In attempting to determine whether a given person is a functional fiduciary with regard to a 401(k) plan, forget about applying any fixed rule. There simply is no bright line test to apply in determining whether one is a fiduciary or is rendering fiduciary type functions with regard to the plan. For these reasons, it becomes even more important for anyone associated with a plan to understand the fiduciary responsibility provisions, as well as the types of activities that might cause a person to be deemed a fiduciary with respect to the plan.

Moreover, it is extremely important to keep sight of the fact that courts have generally interpreted fiduciary status broadly, and continue to broaden the definition to include people once thought to be safely beyond the definition. As a result, many prudent plan advisors, service providers, and company insiders should assume that they are in fact fiduciaries under ERISA and take appropriate measures to ensure that they do not violate ERISA's fiduciary responsibility provisions.

Deciding whether a person has any authority just described is a factual question, demanding an examination of the facts and circumstances of each case. Formal titles are not controlling. Thus, a person's status as a fiduciary depends on his or her function, authority, and responsibility, regardless of that person's own belief about whether he or she is a fiduciary. The test for determining fiduciary status therefore focuses on whether the person exercises any of the functions described earlier and in section 3(21) of ERISA.[106] Examining each function that establishes fiduciary status is instructive.

## Exercise Any Discretionary Authority or Control over the Management of the Plan and/or Its Assets

To date, the regulations issued by the DOL defining fiduciary status do not set forth the conditions that must exist in order for a person to be deemed a fiduciary because of the level of discretionary authority or control they have over

---

106  DOL Reg. §2509.75-8.

the plan's management. However, other interpretative releases, advisory opinions, and court statements indicate who might be deemed a fiduciary because of such discretionary control:

- **Investment committee members and trustees**
  Generally, the individuals serving on the investment committee of a plan who bear the responsibility for managing plan assets and appointing investment managers for the plan are plan fiduciaries under this section. Similarly, plan trustees are fiduciaries because of the nature of their functions with respect to the plan. Trustees who act only on direction generally are held to be fiduciaries but with lessened fiduciary obligation, provided the instructions or lack thereof was in accordance with the plan documents and consistent with ERISA. Such persons routinely perform discretionary responsibilities with regard to the plan.

- **Board of director members**
  Members of the board of directors of any employer that maintains a 401(k) plan will be fiduciaries only to the extent that they personally have responsibility for the discretionary management functions described earlier. For instance, the board of directors might be responsible for the selection and retention of investment managers. In such a case, the board of directors is exercising "discretionary authority or discretionary control respecting the management of the plan" and the directors are therefore, fiduciaries.

- **Other officers and employees**
  Note that an officer or employee of an organization that sponsors a 401(k) plan is not a fiduciary to that plan solely by reason of holding a particular office in the employer's organization if he or she performs none of the discretionary functions noted earlier. An officer or employee will not become a fiduciary unless he or she has or exercises any authority, responsibility, or control over the management of the plan. However, officers and employees of a plan sponsor are fiduciaries if they exercise control through the selection of the investments by means of participation on the investment committee of the plan. Such control might exist even when the officer or employee does not formally sit on the committee but has such influence that he or she effectively controls the committee's actions.

- **Benefit managers**
  Other officers and positions in an organization should always be examined to determine whether they involve the performance of any of the discretionary functions described earlier. For instance, most companies that sponsor 401(k) plans have plan benefit managers who have no

power to make any decisions about plan policy, interpretations, practices, or procedures, but who do perform administrative functions within a preexisting framework of practices and policies made by other plan fiduciaries. Such persons are generally not deemed fiduciaries because they lack any discretionary authority respecting the management of the plan, or the disposition of plan assets. Rather, from the standpoint of ERISA, their functions tend to be ministerial in nature. In addition to ministerial functions, many benefit managers regularly report to plan fiduciaries about certain matters within the discretion of the benefit manager. Such matters might include the preparation of an investment management summary report. As long as the benefit manager does not exercise or participate in the fiduciary decisions, that person is not a plan fiduciary. However, it is commonplace for benefit managers to sit on 401(k) plan committees that determine, for instance, which investment advisory firm will manage the assets under the plan. Such a decision is a fiduciary decision, and to the extent the benefit manager participates in that decision, he or she is a fiduciary of the plan.

- **Attorneys, accountants, and consultants**
  Although the ordinary functions of attorneys, accountants, and other consultants to 401(k) plans (other than as investment advisors) may not at first glance be considered to be fiduciary functions, there will be situations in which such persons may, because of their special expertise or their position, be exercising discretionary control or authority in the management of the plan or its assets. In such situations, it is not at all far-fetched that these persons may be regarded to have assumed fiduciary obligations.

Apart from the apparent situations (that is, those for the trustee, investment committee members, and plan sponsors), the general trend of fiduciary case law has been to test the outer edges of the fiduciary definition. These cases have involved plan service providers who have argued that they are not plan fiduciaries. The trend in these cases appears to be finding fiduciary status where it was not found in earlier cases.

Accordingly, although attorneys, accountants, and other plan consultants performing their usual professional functions will ordinarily not be considered fiduciaries, if the factual situation in a particular case falls within one of the types of conduct noted under section 3(21)(A), such a person may be deemed a fiduciary under the plan.

Additionally, DOL regulations provide that a person who performs purely ministerial functions, for example, clerical functions not requiring the excise of discretion—within the framework of policies, interpretations, rules, practice, and procedures made by other persons—is not a fiduciary.

The DOL lists the following types of ministerial, administrative functions that do not fall within ERISA definition of fiduciary:

- Applying rules to determine eligibility
- Calculating service or compensation credit for benefits
- Preparing employee communication materials
- Maintaining participant service records
- Preparing government agency reports
- Calculating benefits
- Orienting new participants and advising participants or their rights and options under the plan
- Collecting and transmitting contributions as provided in the plan
- Processing claims
- Making recommendations to others for decisions about the plan administration[107]

## Rendering Investment Advice for a Fee or Other Compensation

Section 3(21)(A)(ii) of ERISA provides that any person who renders investment advice to a plan for a fee or other compensation, direct or indirect, or has any authority or responsibility to do so is a fiduciary to the plan. This provision has been interpreted and applied broadly to impose fiduciary status on those persons associated with the investment management of the plan.

The DOL's regulations attempt to specify conditions in which a person would be deemed a fiduciary because of the rendering of investment advice.[108] Generally, a person is rendering investment advice to a plan in a manner that will make that person a fiduciary only if that person does the following:

- Makes recommendations about the valuing, buying, holding, or selling of securities or other property
- Has, directly or indirectly, (a) discretionary authority or control over buying or selling securities or other property for the plan, whether or

---

107 DOL Reg. §2509.75-8.
108 ERISA §3(38).

not pursuant to an agreement, arrangement, or understanding; or (b) regularly renders advice to a plan pursuant to a mutual agreement, arrangement, or understanding that such advice will serve as one of the primary bases for the investment of plan assets and that this advice will be based on the particular needs of the plan from the standpoint of investment policy, strategy, diversification, or portfolio composition

In other words, merely rendering investment advice is not enough to make a person a fiduciary of a plan. In order for a person to be considered a plan fiduciary, the investment advice must be given to the plan for a fee or other compensation. In addition, for a person who is rendering investment advice to a plan for a fee to be a fiduciary of the plan, that person must have some level of actual control over buying or selling securities for the plan or must be operating within an agreement or understanding that this advice will be used to make investment decisions.

## Consultants, Agents, Brokers, and Salespersons

A more difficult question arises concerning whether the people who suggest or recommend investment vehicles to the 401(k) plan are fiduciaries. Such people might include pension consultants, mutual fund representatives, insurance agents, investment management consultants, or brokers. As a practical matter, any advice and recommendations made by these people to plans and plan fiduciaries about the advisability of investing in, purchasing, or selling securities; hiring or firing an investment manager; or otherwise selecting an investment vehicle for the 401(k) plan could constitute investment advice so that the persons who furnish such advice could be classified as fiduciaries under certain circumstances.

These circumstances must include, as noted earlier, the payment of a fee or other compensation to such a person, either directly or indirectly. This includes, for example, brokerage commissions, mutual fund sales commissions, insurance sales commissions, and consulting fees.

In addition, because they ordinarily would not have discretion or control over plan assets, these people can be deemed fiduciaries only by virtue of their rendering of investment advice to the plan. As mentioned previously, in order for someone to be considered a plan fiduciary, he or she must offer such advice within a context wherein it is expected that the fiduciary will rely on the advice in making various plan investment decisions.

In this way, some investment brokers have been deemed fiduciaries because of their purported influence over plan clients, even though the brokers technically had no discretionary power over plan assets. In a particular instance, a stockbroker's recommendations were routinely rubber-stamped by the plan trustees.[109] Thus, even though the broker lacked actual discretionary authority, his advice was routinely followed with the tacit understanding that it would form an important basis for the fiduciary's investment decisions. Thus, the court found that he had effectively exercised authority because of his influence over the client and therefore had achieved fiduciary status.

In such instances, the person is said to render investment advice because he or she makes recommendations about buying or selling securities and regularly renders advice with the understanding that it will serves as a primary basis for plan investment decisions. Thus, a broker's practice of merely recommending investments should not make that broker a fiduciary in the absence of any agreement, arrangement, or understanding referred to above. However, to the extent a plan fiduciary can be shown to rely very heavily on a broker's recommendations, such as an understanding can be inferred, and the broker could theoretically be deemed a fiduciary.

## Plan Administrators

One confusing title used in ERISA is the plan administrator. ERISA requires every plan to designate a plan administrator within the plan instrument. When such a designation is absent, ERISA designates the employer-sponsor as the plan administrator.

It should be noted that the plan administrator as designated under ERISA is not the same thing as the same term used to describe participant record-keeping or actuarial functions. Such people, although performing administrative functions, are technically not plan administrators as defined under ERISA.

In general, the actual plan administrator so designated under the plan will have certain responsibilities for making decisions with respect to eligibility and other such functions. In any event, the plan administrator of any plan is a fiduciary by definition under ERISA section 3(21).

In conclusion, any people with influence or power respecting the management of the plan need to be cognizant of their potential status as fiduciaries. As the impact of the regulations becomes clearer through practice and litigation, it is becoming clear that bodies charged with enforcement of ERISA are anxious to paint as many people as possible with the fiduciary brush, and the courts are beginning to fashion a body of law along these lines. Accordingly, it is always best to be well aware of lines of conduct governing a fiduciary's activities, even if one does not consider oneself a fiduciary.

---

109  Reich v. McManus, 883 F Supp. 1144 (ND Ill 1995).

# PROHIBITED TRANSACTIONS UNDER ERISA

Under ERISA and the Internal Revenue Code, certain classes of transactions are prohibited between a plan and parties-in-interest. These transactions are prohibited regardless of the terms of the transaction and whether it provides economic or other benefit to the plan. In addition to these technically prohibited transactions, plan fiduciaries are also prohibited under ERISA from engaging in any transaction or conduct that would jeopardize their duty of loyalty to the plan. Plan fiduciaries and their advisors must be aware of these particular restrictions because even an inadvertent violation can subject the party-in-interest and the fiduciary to serve penalties.

Specifically, under ERISA section 406, a prohibited transaction occurs if a plan fiduciary causes the plan to enter into any of the following transactions with a party-in-interest:

- Sale, exchange, or lease of property
- Loan or extension of credit
- Transfer of plan assets or use of plan assets
- Acquisition of employer securities or employer real property in excess of certain limits
- In addition to these specific prohibitions, ERISA focuses on self-dealing and conflict of interests by prohibiting a plan fiduciary from doing any of the following:
  o Dealing with plan assets in the fiduciary's own interest
  o Representing adverse interests in any transaction with the plan,
  o Receiving remuneration in any form from a party dealing with the
  o plan in connection with a transaction involving plan assets

The penalties for violating these prohibited transaction provisions can be extreme. Under the Internal Revenue Code, the IRS can impose a penalty tax on the party-in-interest to the transaction equal to five percent of the amount involved in the transaction for each year the transaction remains uncorrected. An additional tax of 100 percent can be imposed if the transaction is not corrected in a timely manner.

To the extent that a plan fiduciary engages in a prohibited transaction, the plan fiduciary is personally liable for making up any losses to the plan or for providing to the plan any profit earned through use of the plan assets. The DOL may also impose civil penalties on the plan fiduciary.

## Party-In-Interest

A party-in-interest is defined under section 3(14) of ERISA to include any of the following:

1. Any fiduciary, administrator, trustee, counsel, or employee of the plan
2. Any person providing services to the plan
3. Any employer whose employees are covered by the plan, as well as any 50 percent owner of the employer
4. Any relative (spouse, ancestor, or lineal descendent) of the persons described in items 1, 2, and 3
5. Any employee organization some of whose members are covered by the plan
6. Any entity of which at least 50 percent is owned by any of the five categories just mentioned
7. Any officers, directors, or shareholders who hold 10 percent or more of shares, and employees of any person or company described in items 2, 3, 5 or 6
8. Partners of 10 percent or more of items 2, 3, 5, or 6

The purpose of the prohibited transaction rules is to prevent so-called insiders from using their influence over the plan to cause the plan to engage in a transaction under which they can personally benefit at the expense of the plan. The opportunity for abuse is too great to allow any transactions with the plan except under certain narrow circumstances because of the relationship these persons have to the plan.

## Statutory and Administrative Exemptions

In some instances, ERISA specifically allows certain transactions that might otherwise have been prohibited, providing that the transactions meet the following conditions:

- Certain loans to participants and beneficiaries
- Necessary plan services for reasonable compensation
- Loans to employee stock ownership plans
- Ancillary services provided by a bank
- Acquisition or sale of qualifying employer securities[110]

---

110 ERISA §408.

All of these statutory exemptions are subject to comprehensive regulations and conditions. Interested readers are referred to the DOL's regulations on this subject.

In addition to statutory exemptions under ERISA, the DOL is permitted to issue administrative exemptions to permit specific transactions that are technically prohibited under section 406. In essence, DOL is permitted to issue an administrative exemption if it is (1) administratively feasible, (2) in the best interest of the plan and its participants and beneficiaries, and (3) protective of the rights of participants and beneficiaries.[111] The administrative procedures required gaining and administrative exemptions are complex and should only be undertaken with qualified ERISA counsel.

Finally, there are a number of class exemptions issued by the DOL that automatically provide relief to any party-in-interest and plan fiduciary that meet the specific criteria set forth in the exemption. These class exemptions cover a variety of common transactions and should be consulted with the assistance of qualified counsel. In summary, the prohibited transaction provisions are technical landmines. Plan fiduciaries must be extremely careful not to engage in such transactions regardless of their intentions and any economic or other benefit to the plan.

---

111  Prohibited Transaction Exemptions (PTE) 96-62.

# Chapter 8—INVESTMENT MANAGEMENT IN 401(k) PLANS

Among the components of a 401(k) plan, investment management has generally received less attention than participant record keeping and communications. It appears that with the shift from employer-directed to participant-directed plans came a diminished focus on one of the most important aspects of the plan—its investment options. Nonetheless, given the growing number of investment options available, better participant education and therefore greater investment sophistication, plus a recent influx of fiduciary breach lawsuits related to investments the selection and monitoring of investments are gaining the attention of plan sponsors.

Companies have just begun to develop their own practices for managing fiduciary responsibilities in these plans. It is clear that the plan fiduciary has the same, if not greater, responsibilities in the selection and oversight of participant-directed plan investment managers as he or she does for any employer-directed plan. Through out this chapter, five steps function as a common theme. They are: (1) analyze current position; (2) diversify or allocate asserts or investment options; (3) formalize and document investment policy and procedures; (4) Implement the policy; and (5) Monitor and supervise the process, and readjust when necessary.

**Figure 8-1: The Investment Management Process**

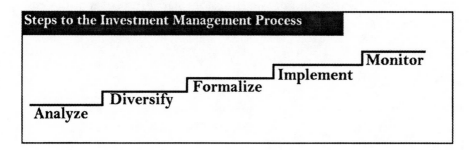

Giving participants investment choices imposes on plan sponsors the same daunting responsibility in overseeing the investment options in participant-directed plans. Although participants are ultimately responsible for their investment decisions, they have taken action against their employer for not offering a suitable range of investment options. As these plans mature and participants begin to receive distributions, those plan sponsors who engaged in a rigorous manager selection and review process should be protected from frivolous employee litigation.

This chapter explores and suggests standards for plan sponsors to follow as they select and monitor investment managers for their 401(k) plans. Although some of these practices may seem like a heavy burden to place on the plan sponsor, ERISA requires that "care, skill, prudence, and diligence"[112] be used in the investment decision process. Regardless of whether the plan seeks a full-service, bundled product, or investment management services alone, there are standards of prudence for proper management of plan assets.

# TYPES OF INVESTMENT VEHICLES

At a minimum, plan sponsors should offer participants a range of investment options that has enough diversity in its risk and reward characteristics to satisfy the requirements of 404(c). Essentially, this means that the plan's investment options should be diverse enough to allow participants to construct their own portfolios covering unique asset classes. The objective is to put participants in a position where they can maximize their performance while minimizing risk through diversification of asset classes. As such, it is critical that plan sponsors retain a degree of oversight to ensure that the range of options does not become overweighed in one investment style or another. Fortunately, for plan sponsors, there is a wide array of investment options available for 401(k) plans, with more product development occurring as participant-directed plans gain in popularity and participants become investors that are more sophisticated.

---

112   ERISA §404(a)(1)(B).

## Figure 8-2: Risk and Reward Traits of Common Investment Vehicles

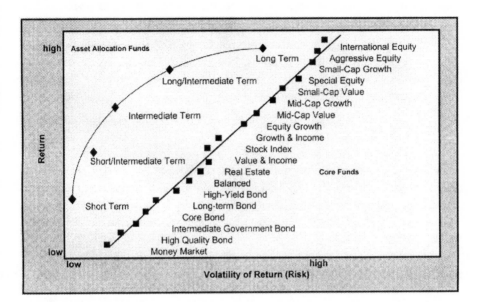

## Mutual Funds

Mutual funds have become extremely popular as investment options in participant-directed 401(k) plans. In its August 2004 article, "401(k) Plan Asset Allocations, Account Balances, and Loans Accounting in 2003", the Investment Company Institute (ICI) reported that mutual fund companies were the leading providers of investment management services to 401(k) plans. Several characteristics of mutual funds make them attractive as 401(k) plan options:

- Many plan participants understand mutual funds and may have invested in them outside their 401(k) plan. Participants take comfort in the fact that they can follow fund performance in the newspaper and generally feel familiar with the way these investments operate.

- Mutual funds range in investment objective from stable, fixed-income funds to aggressive growth funds, so plan sponsors can find mutual fund choices to suit virtually any participant population's investment needs.

- Many mutual fund companies offer "ready-mixed" asset allocation or "lifestyle" funds for participants who do not want to create their own investment strategy. These funds have become extremely popular because they allow participants who lack investment expertise to invest in all three asset classes, minimize their risk, and use more effective long-term investment strategies than they might create on their own.

- Mutual fund companies have developed record-keeping technology and shareholder communications to provide participants with a fair amount of regular information, including shareholder reports, performance figures, and updated prospectuses, which may help satisfy the "sufficient information" requirements of 404(c).

- The systems capability of many mutual fund vendors lends itself well to daily participant record keeping.[113]

Because the features of mutual funds are so attractive to 401(k) plan participants, the demand for them as investment options has increased significantly during the last ten years. According to the ICI, in 2003 401(k) plan assets in mutual funds were at $349 billion, which accounted for 45 percent of the total 401(k) market.

## Bank Collective Funds

Another commonly used investment vehicle in 401(k) plans is the bank collective fund, which is exempt from registration requirements under federal securities law. These collective funds have relatively low internal operating costs and are not subject to some of the restrictions that are applicable to registered mutual funds. Thus, some people feel they offer investment flexibility and an enhanced ability to respond to immediate market pressures. The disadvantage of using collective funds is that their unit values are not normally listed in newspapers. Accordingly, participants tend to be less familiar and less comfortable with collective funds as investment vehicles in their 401(k) accounts.

## Insurance Company Separate Accounts

Insurance company separate accounts are most frequently used by small 401(k) plans. These investments are similar to mutual funds and collective funds in that they are commingled investment vehicles and generally well diversified. As with collective funds, separate accounts suffer a perception disadvantage because they are not listed in the newspaper. As a result, participants may be uncomfortable with a vehicle they do not understand. Further, separate accounts normally are loaded with a variety of fees that can be difficult to identify and understand.

---

113  Investment Company Institute, 2004 Mutual Fund Fact Book.

## Separate Account Management

Plans with total assets over several million dollars often consider the separate account management services provided by many independent investment managers. The ICI reports that 40 percent of plans with more than 4,000 participants or $50 million in assets use separate account management.[114] Under a separate account management arrangement, the investment manager would create a private fund for each investment category determined by the plan. A consultant or financial advisor can work with the plan sponsor to determine the most suitable separate accounts, given plan parameters and the participant population. Like mutual funds, separate accounts can be created as asset allocation strategies, where the investment manager will spread the assets among stocks, bonds, and cash. This type of account offers the benefits of diversification and asset allocation to participants who are uncomfortable "mixing" individual investment options to create an effective long-term allocation.

Separate account management offers the advantage of custom-tailored investment options, such that the plan fiduciaries and their advisors can specify with great clarity the investment objectives of each fund. The funds can be managed according to specific objectives set by the plan because they are not commingled with any other plans. Further, plan sponsors and their advisors can monitor these accounts in accordance with any custom-designed indexes or benchmarks they deem appropriate.

As with collective funds and insurance company separate accounts, the separate account unit values are not listed in the newspaper, which can be disconcerting to plan participants. In addition, separate account management can sometimes cause some administrative difficulties with daily valuation and processing exchanges among other plan options.

## Employer Stock

Many plan sponsors offer their company stock as an investment option for their 401(k) plans. Although employer stock is generally considered a more aggressive growth option, it can be attractive to participants because it allows them to have ownership in their organization. Moreover, service providers have developed both record-keeping services and technology to allow them to efficiently handle the administrative aspects of company stock as an investment option. Depending on the accounting methods used for company stock valuation, participants may or may not be able to track the performance in the newspaper. If the stock is

---

114 Investment Company Institute, 401(k) Plans: How Plan Sponsors See the Marketplace (Winter 1995).

valued using unit accounting, the unit value is not published in the newspaper; however, if the company stock is valued using share accounting, participants have a better chance of tracking performance on a daily basis.

## Self-Directed Brokerage Account (SBA)

With the shift to a more dynamic, robust environment, the self-directed brokerage account has become a growing investment option in 401(k) plans. Plansponsor.com reflects in its 2003 Defined Contribution Survey, that approximately twenty-two percent of plans offer an SBA option. A SBA allows participants to invest in virtually any publicly traded asset instead of being limited to a group of preselected funds.

# FINDING THE BEST INVESTMENT OPTIONS

Although all of the options discussed above have their advantages and disadvantages, there is not one perfect option. Instead, plan sponsors should consider how the features of the various options might meet the unique needs of their plan and participants. For example, the simplicity and acceptability of registered mutual funds might be appealing to a particular employee population. Otherwise, for participants requiring a focused investment strategy, tapping into a particular area of investment expertise through separate account management can provide more customized options. Generally, asset distribution in 401(k) plans is undergoing a shift from heavy concentration in fixed-income options to equity options. Given the decline in interest rates that occurred between 1994 and 2004, windows of outstanding stock market performance, and better participant education, plan sponsors have experienced increased demand for more investment options, particularly in the equity area. In the last year, more than half the plan sponsors who added investment options to their plans added growth and aggressive growth options. Applying the standards explained in the previous chapter, the following figure illustrates the duties of a fiduciary to investment management.

### Figure 8-3: Fiduciary Standards for Investment Management

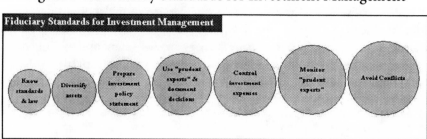

# THE INVESTMENT POLICY STATEMENT

Just as a journey requires a roadmap, a 401(k) plan requires a clearly articulated set of directions for selecting and monitoring investment options. Plan sponsors can create and enforce these guidelines by establishing an investment policy statement. Unfortunately, although an investment policy statement is almost a perfunctory requirement in employer-directed plans, few 401(k) plan sponsors have thought it necessary in order to manage their fiduciary responsibilities. This is yet another symptom of many plan sponsors' misconceptions about their responsibilities in participant-directed plans.

Certainly, we now know that from a fiduciary standpoint, there is no legal distinction between employer-and participant-directed plans. Just as plan fiduciaries have established investment policy statements in their employer-directed plans, they now must establish similar guidelines to govern the investment manager selections and monitoring process in their participant-directed plans. In fact, it is entirely likely that an investment policy statement is even more important in a participant-directed plan because the plan sponsors are in effect absolving themselves of day-to-day investment allocation decisions in participants' own accounts.

Section 401(b)(1) of ERISA requires that every employee benefit plan shall "provide a procedure for establishing and carrying out a funding policy and method consistent with the objectives of the plan and the requirements of this title."[115] Therefore, plan sponsors must force discipline into the investment process by building a framework of investment options that can stand up to scrutiny at any point in time. The best way to do this is to create a clearly articulated policy with standards against which both the investment options and managers can be measured.

Consider the possibilities when no investment policy statement is used. If either a disgruntled participant or the U.S. Department of Labor (DOL) were to raise a claim of imprudent selection and monitoring under ERISA, a court reviewing such a claim would want to see evidence of the fiduciary's conduct in the investment management process. Without a written investment policy statement, the investment selection process might appear haphazard. In contrast, the presence of an investment policy statement lends credence to the fiduciary's position that he or she has engaged in a through selection process, as evidenced by the fact that a written document was prepared to govern this systematic process. If an investment policy statement is not reduced to writing, it is not mutually understood; and the absence of understanding between the

---

115 ERISA §401(b)(1).

supervising fiduciaries and the investment professionals serving the trust is the most significant cause of not attaining the investment objectives.

As a practical matter, an investment policy statement is a written statement of the goals of the plan and the rules to be followed by the money managers to achieve those goals.

Essentially the investment policy statement is the navigational chart that the plan sponsor establishes to first select and then guide the investment managers of the plan. The investment policy statement can also establish performance targets, risk parameters, communications objectives, and policies.

## Establishing the Investment Policy Statement in a Participant-Directed Plan

Because the employees, not the plan sponsor, make the investment allocation decisions, the investment policy statement for the participant-directed plan will bear little resemblance to that of defined-benefit or even employer-directed defined contribution plans. Thus, the investment policy statement should focus on the steps necessary to ensure that participants' rights and interest are protected as specified under section 404(c) and relevant ERISA case law and regulations. Further, the policy statement should emphasize the required actions of the plan fiduciaries to ensure that the participants are indeed in control of their assets.

Creating the investment policy statement should be a cooperative process, involving both the company's human resource and treasury professionals as well as the chosen investment manager. An interactive discussion about what options would be best for the plan, given its participant population and administrative parameters, should follow. Once created, the individuals responsible for its establishment should review this investment policy at least annually. Building an investment policy should involve creating a partnership between the plan sponsor and the investment manager. Additionally, Plansponsor.com in their 2003 Defined Contribution Survey indicate that 67.3 percent of plans have a written investment policy statement.

### Step 1: Identify the Responsible Fiduciaries
The first step toward establishing the investment policy should be to determine who is responsible for the management of various aspects of the plan. The regulations issued under section 404(c) of ERISA inherently require a responsible fiduciary to designate investment managers and/or options under the plan. This fiduciary cannot have any affiliation with the investment management organization that is managing the assets. Thus, under normal circumstances the

plan fiduciary will be a person who is employed by the plan sponsor. These regulations impose on the fiduciary the continuing obligation to assess the suitability of and prudently monitor the chose investment managers.

## Step 2: Determine the Types of Investment Options under the Plan

The process of selecting investment options for the plan should include the input of all plan fiduciaries as well as consultants or financial advisors. Before the actual selection of investment options can take place, there should be a formal adoption of the policy that will govern the range of investments to be offered under the plan.

The guiding light for the selection of investment options should be the section 404(c) regulations that require participants to be given a "broad range" of investment alternatives with varying risk and return characteristics. Nevertheless, it is equally important to consider (1) depth of investment knowledge of participants, (2) risk tolerance of participants, (3) size of plan, (4) plan design features, (5) cost considerations, and (6) liquidity needs, in selecting options for the plan. Therefore, the investment policy should include the following directives:

- The range of options should include at least five or six vehicles that vary significantly in their reactions to market and economic conditions. An adequately broad range might include: (1) a guaranteed investment contract (GIC) or money market fund; (2) a broad-based bond fund; (3) a conservative equity fund (domestic); (4) an international equity fund; (5) an aggressive equity fund; and (6) an asset allocation or lifestyle fund.

- Participants should have options with enough diversity in the risk and return characteristics such that they can make prudent and suitable investment decisions for their own portfolios.

- Participants should receive a reasonable opportunity to materially affect the potential returns as well as the ability to control risk in their accounts through diversification.

By incorporating these directives, plan fiduciaries can ensure that the plan offers an adequate range of investment options for participants at the same time, they can identify categories and ultimately particular options to be offered under the plan.

## Step 3: Set Investment Performance Criteria and Risk Parameters

Although many 401(k) plan sponsors have not focused seriously on investment performance in their plans, establishing written investment performance objectives and risk parameters will help them conduct due diligence and careful monitoring. Plan sponsors should consider both quantitative and qualitative factors. Quantitative factors include: (1) relative performance record versus designated benchmarks, similar advisors, risk/return measures, and track record quality; (2) consistency of investment style and discipline; and (3) consistency of performance through market cycles. Qualitative factors include: (1) organization and fiscal strength, client services, compliance and legal, operations and negative press; (2) qualification and consistency of investment management personnel; (3) clear and concise investment philosophy; and (4) trading capabilities with 401(k) record keeper and trustee.

Establishing variable investment performance standards requires a sophisticated knowledge of capital markets and the relationship between investment returns and volatility. Most fiduciaries of 401(k) plans gain considerably by retaining a qualified consultant or financial advisor to help them formulate performance standards and determine risk parameters.

Furthermore, when establishing target investment returns, plan sponsors must understand the relationship between investment returns and risk. Risk is generally defined in terms of volatility, that is, the frequency and amount that an investment fluctuates (or deviates) from its average return. The more an investment deviates from that return, the more volatile (risky) it is, despite the fact that the investment might produce above-average returns.

Volatility is commonly measured through standard deviation, reflecting the range of price fluctuations likely for a particular investment. Most studies of standard deviation indicate that equities generally exhibit higher standard deviations than do bonds. Within the different types of equities, there is a wide range of standard deviations depending on industry groups, company particulars, and a variety of other market factors.

To establish investment performance standards in either absolute or relative terms, the investment policy must also clearly articulate appropriate risk parameters. The responsibility to quantify risk is virtually mandated under section 404(c), as noted earlier.

### Step 4: Determine Performance Measurement Standards

Performance measurement standards should be made in conjunction with the establishment of performance objectives. Because most 401(k) plans today offer at least four investment options, the investment policy statement needs to identify the appropriate benchmarks for measuring investment performance in each respective category. Service providers and/or consultants or financial advisors can work with plan sponsors to determine appropriate benchmarks for each asset category and, where appropriate, for individual options. Although performance measurement is discussed later in this chapter, for purposes of the investment policy statement there must be an identification of the indices that will be used as long-and short-term performance measurement standards.

The plan may adopt a variety of performance measurements. For instance, it may be appropriate to compare one stock portfolio to an index of growth stock portfolios. In a balanced fund, it may be appropriate to compare segments of the fund to referenced benchmarks on a nominal basis (for example, comparing the stock component to an index of relevant stock portfolios). Using indices appropriate for different segments of a fund will have more meaning than a single numeric comparison. In any event, there should be a consensus on which benchmark indices and what period will be used to measure investment performance for each fund.

Recent trends of DOL audits and participant scrutiny reflect a growing concern on fees. Although ERISA does not set a specific level of fees, it does require fees charged to the plan be reasonable. Moreover, reasonable must be determined on a case-by-case basis. When evaluating fees plan sponsors should make informed decisions, remember fees are just one of several factors, assess the plan's performance over time for each investment option, look at the full value of services, consider all plan fees, not just fund expenses, and remember choosing lower fees does not necessarily mean a better performing fund. An additional consideration related to fees is to remember that some investments, due to their nature, may have higher fees. In short, as long as expense ratios and fees are reasonable, the selection process should be guided by appropriate measures of performance versus risk, not by shaving a few points on the expense ratio.

## Step 5: Determine Manager Termination Procedures

The investment policy statement must articulate the conditions that will lead to manager termination or other corrective action and the procedures to follow when these conditions exist. Therefore, this is an extremely important matter because of the fiduciary liability risk associated with failing to take corrective measures when there is evidence of problems. As noted earlier, the fiduciaries have an ongoing duty to assess the suitability of the designated investment managers and the further responsibility to take corrective measures when the suitability of any of the selected managers is in question.

## Step 6: Establish Participant Control Parameters

Because participant-directed plans must allow participants to exercise control over their assets, it is appropriate to articulate the standards or parameters of control as a matter of investment policy. Following DOL's regulations, the investment policy statement should dictate the following requirements pertaining to participant control:[116]

---

116 ERISA §404(c).

- Participants should be given reasonable opportunity to give investment instructions to an identified plan fiduciary that is obliged to carry out these instructions.

- The plan may impose on the trust asset charges for reasonable expenses associated with the opportunity to exercise control, if participants are informed of this policy.

- Plan fiduciaries may decline to implement participant instructions under the conditions specified in the regulations.

- The plan may impose reasonable restrictions on the frequency of investment instructions, provided such restrictions are uniformly applied to all participants and provided further that participants are given the ability to give instructions with such frequency as is appropriate given the volatility of the investment options as governed under the section 404(c) regulations.

- With respect to the three core investments constituting the broad selection of investment options under the plan, participants are given the ability to give investment instructions once every three months.

To ensure that all plan fiduciaries fully understand the essence of participant control, the investment policy statement should indicate that participant control over assets is absent when (1) the participant is subjected to improper influence by the fiduciary or plan sponsor, (2) a plan fiduciary has concealed material nonpublic facts, or (3) the participant is legally incompetent and the plan fiduciary knows of this condition.[117]

### Step 7: Establish Participant Communications Policies

The investment policy statement should include policies concerning communication of investment information because effective participant communication is integral to the success of a participant-directed 401(k) plan. Where communications are deficient, fiduciary liability may result if it is determined that participants did not have control over their plan investments. Thus, as a means of limiting fiduciary liability, it is critical to include a participant communications policy to articulate the standards that will govern investment-related communications.

This statement should dictate, among other things, the methods and timing of communications, the nature of communication devices, and policies concerning the permissibility to render investment advice to participants. In

---

117  DOL Reg. §2550.404c-1(c)(2)

the absence of a special prohibited transaction exception from the DOL, ERISA prohibits investment management organizations from giving investment advice to plan participants because of the potential for conflicts of interest.

# THE FUND SELECTION PROCESS

In many ways, the 401(k) industry continues to be in its infancy with respect to the manager selection process. Consulting firms who have dominated the defined benefit investment manager search process have only begun to develop expertise in the area of 401(k). As a result, decisions are often made based on who makes the best presentation rather than on ability. With the multitude of investment managers and the growing complexity of the investment process, plan sponsors are beginning to recognize the need for independent expertise. The level of knowledge needed to select and monitor a 401(k) plan's investment options is normally beyond most plan sponsors' experience. In general, the process should include: data gathering, quantitative screens to score and rank each product, conduct due diligence research, and evaluate and assign ratings to each product. The following provides an overview of the selection process.

**Figure 8-4: The Selection Process**

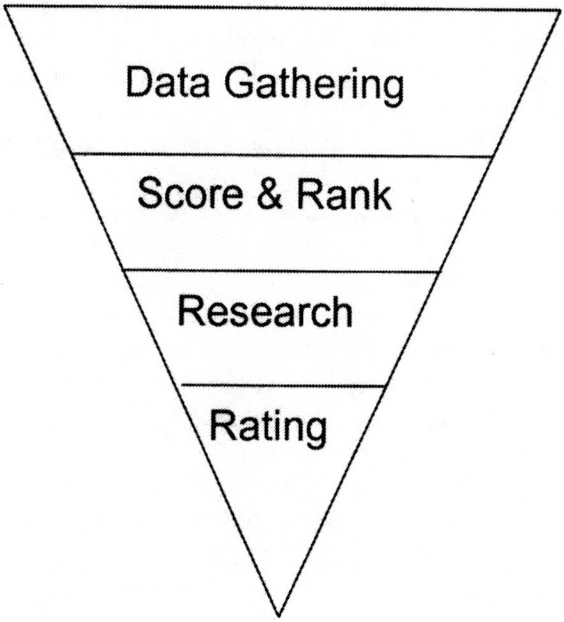

## Seek Outside Expertise: Hire a Consultant or Financial Advisor or Advisor

A consultant or financial advisor's expertise can support plan sponsors in the fulfillment of their fiduciary responsibilities. More specifically, a consultant, financial advisor, or other advisor can assist the plan sponsor with the following:

- Establish investment policy statement
- Understand and determine appropriate investment management styles in the plan
- Understand and determine risk parameters
- Evaluate and select investment managers
- Monitor the performance and volatility of the funds
- Provide continuing due diligence
- Evaluate participant record-keeping capabilities
- Evaluate and customize participant communication programs

## Establish Plan Asset Categories

The factors that will determine both asset category and individual investment option selection include (1) depth of investment knowledge of participants, (2) risk tolerance of participants, (3) size of plan, (4) plan design features, (5) cost considerations, and (6) liquidity needs. The partnership between the plan sponsor and service provider is critical to this selection process given the importance of input from the plan sponsor's treasury and human resources areas, and the service provider's understanding of the plan's investment needs.

Most 401(k) plans today limit participants to several investment options that have been preselected by the plan fiduciaries. According to a survey conducted in 2003 by the Profit Sharing/401(k) Council of America (PSCA), 87 percent of plan sponsors offer ten or more mutual fund choices, with the average being sixteen.[118] The trend to increase the number of options beyond the traditional core investment categories is generally attributable to declining interest rates, good stock market performance, robust Internet technology, and better participant education programs.

In recent years, participants have asked for more help with their investment decisions. While investment education points the way, it does not give answers

---

118  Profit Sharing/401(k) Council of America (PSCA), 47th Annual Survey of Profit Sharing and 401(k) Plans (2003).

to participant questions about specific amounts in options. Providing investment advice through a third-party registered investment advisor may help participants make more informed and productive decisions.

Additionally, both media focus and plan sponsor concern about retirement risk, such as arriving at retirement without enough money on which to live, has prompted considerable emphasis on teaching participants to be investors rather than just savers. As such, it becomes even more critical for plan sponsors to provide a range of options that makes it possible for participants to create appropriate allocations based on their own needs.

Considering the pool of 401(k) assets to be a pie, the asset allocation decisions will happen on two levels. First, the plan sponsor must determine the composition or ingredients of the pie. This requires a careful analysis of whether various asset categories and investment styles will effectively work together in numerous different allocations. Second, the participants will carve up the pie, making their own actual investment allocation decisions.

At a minimum, the plan's investment options should include at least one selection from the following categories:

- Stable value
- Fixed income
- Domestic stock (value and growth)
- International or foreign stock

## Asset Allocation and Combining Investment Styles

Plan sponsors should choose investment options from each of the aforementioned categories because certain combinations of styles create more effective asset allocation than do others. For instance, if a plan were limited to three investment options consisting of a money market fund, a GIC fund, and employer stock, the plan participants would be hampered in their ability to maximize investment returns while reducing risk. Moreover, such a selection would not satisfy the broad selection criteria of section 404(c). However, a participant that had access to aggressive growth, value, bond, and stable value investment options could create a more effective combination of investment styles, and therefore a more desirable allocation.

As an investment theory, asset allocation is a valid principle. Studies have shown that allocating assets among investment categories is far more important to investment returns than actually choosing the right stocks or bonds. In fact, over 90 percent of the movement in an investment portfolio is the result of strategic asset allocation (long-term exposure to a broad range of asset classes), whereas only 10 percent is the result of the actual stock selection.

In addition to strategic asset allocation, there is also tactical asset allocation, which refers to the movement of money between the asset classes, specifically, tactically shifting the asset mix. It is important not to confuse asset allocation with diversification. Diversification as a basic principle seeks to reduce risk and increase returns by spreading investments across asset categories that historically have performed differently from one another.

The asset allocation strategy can create a serious dilemma for employees because many may be ill equipped to make these decisions. In a study of more than 1,000 randomly selected plan participants, only 26 percent believed that they were well qualified to make investment decisions for themselves.[119] Only eight percent of sponsors believed that employees were well qualified to make their own investment decisions. Hence, employee communications and education programs are critical to participants' ability to make informed investment decisions. Suggestions for effective participant communications are described in Chapter 10.

Strategic asset allocation should be a long-term decision. Participants should be encouraged to ride through the inevitable ups and downs in the portfolio with the knowledge that in the long run they will do better than trying to time the market. Further, participants must understand that passively maintained steady allocations will require periodic adjustments. For instance, if a participant were exercising asset allocation in her his/her portfolio with a 65 percent equity commitment, market appreciation or depreciation over time will change the percentage that the participant actually has invested in equities relative to the other categories. Thus, this participant would need to adjust the balance in his/her accounts in order to maintain a long-term strategic allocation of 65 percent equities.

For participants who simply do not wish to make their own asset allocation decisions, there are a growing number of asset allocation or lifestyle funds available as investment options. Because these funds are virtually tailor-made for 401(k) plan participants, who generally have limited investment experience, plan sponsors should consider adding some type of asset allocation option to their plan. Asset allocation funds take all of the complex issues behind making investment decisions and boil them down to one simple strategy. In addition, these funds are created to target various investor strategies. Larger plans may also consider having an investment manager create a tailor-made asset allocation strategy as a separately managed account.

---

119 Scarborough Group, 401k Participant Study.

# INVESTMENT MANAGER STYLES

There is more to successfully selecting investment managers in 401(k) plans than simply selecting equity, bond, and balanced mutual funds. Because there are a variety of styles in each asset category, plan sponsors must determine which investment styles would be appropriate for their plans. Once again, this task should precede the actual selection of investment managers. In fact, by making these decisions in advance, plan sponsors may save themselves considerable time by avoiding interviews with asset managers whose style is inappropriate to the plan's investment policy and objectives.

## Active versus Passive Management

Because active investment management consistently outperforms market indices over time, most plan sponsors choose actively managed options over passively managed investments. Active managers essentially try to beat market returns by making intelligent buy-and-sell decisions based on their investment discipline and market and economic outlooks. In contrast, passive management attempts merely to mirror the investment returns in the market. The most common form of passive management is indexing, in which a basket of securities is purchased in an effort to precisely mirror some popular index such as the Standard and Poor's 500, Wilshire 5000, or Russell 2000. Indexing became extremely popular and successful during the 1980s, but index funds are generally valid only during sustained bull markets.

## Value Managers and Contrarian Managers

Value managers look for stocks whose current market price is substantially less than what the managers believe the stocks' actual value should be. Value stocks are characterized by low price-to-earnings ratio (which may result from investor disappointment) and often by high dividend yields. Typically, these are stocks of companies that the market has overlooked, whether because of a slump in business or lack of publicity. Generally, the market has low expectations for these stocks, which is why value managers can buy them at such low prices. Eventually (it is assumed), value stocks become attractive as the expectations trading activity rise.

Because value stocks can provide both current income and long-term capital appreciation, the value management style is appropriate for plans that seek long-term total return. Value managers tend to perform better than the market when the market is trending down, while providing close-to-market returns in a rising equity market. During a market cycle, the objective of a value manager generally is to equal or exceed market returns with less risk.

To choose companies in which to invest, value managers focus on the following:

- Companies with anticipated growth in earnings per share, increasing dividends, or excess cash flow
- Medium to large capitalization stocks
- Companies with sound balance sheets
- Companies with lower-than-market price-to-earnings multiple with a moderate to high dividend yield

Contrarian managers are an extreme form of value managers. Their focus is on the stocks of companies that are out of favor, so a contrarian manager theoretically purchases stocks that are priced much lower than their actual value. Generally, contrarian managers will expect to perform well in down markets and should participate well in up markets.

## Growth Managers

Generally a more aggressive approach than value management, the growth management style focuses on investments whose future potential for growth exceeds the expectation for the market in general. Growth managers invest in the stocks of companies with earnings that are growing faster than the market average and are expected to continue to grow rapidly in the future. Generally, growth managers tend to focus on the following:

- Companies with high current and expected earnings-per-share growth, and momentum
- Small-to medium-sized companies with high-quality ratings and high financial advantage
- Companies with low dividend yields and high price-to-earnings ratios

As an investment style, growth management is a suitable choice for plans looking for long-term returns mostly through principal appreciation. Participants who use this type of option must be able to ride out significant fluctuations in value typically associated with growth stocks, in order to take advantage of higher potential returns.

Within the growth management style, there is aggressive management that focuses on the following:

- Non-Standard and Poor's 500 and smaller capitalization companies with accelerating earnings per share
- Companies that are highly leveraged, have high price-to-earnings ratios, and low or no dividends

Aggressive growth funds are most suitable for investors with extremely high-risk tolerance and who are seeking appreciation. As an investment style, aggressive growth selections can perform well in up markets but generally do poorly in down markets. For this reason, it is important for participants who select this type of option to have a long-term investment period.

## Asset Allocation/Balance Managers

Asset allocation or balanced managers function in part as both strategic and tactical asset allocators, shifting holdings among stocks, bonds, and cash, depending on their evaluations and predictions of economic and market conditions. In many respects, this management style, as discussed previously, offers investors one-stop shopping, and is an option ideally suited for 401(k) plan participants. The asset allocation or balanced management style has the following characteristics:

- Global investment and economic perspectives
- Utilization of both growth and value styles, including small—and large-capitalization companies
- Strategically weighted investments in stocks, bonds, and cash
- Management capabilities within a variety of investment styles

As an investment category, asset allocation or balanced managers may incorporate different investment styles. For instance, some managers focus on value stocks within the general category of equities, whereas others might focus more heavily on growth companies. In either event, this type of option makes inherent sense in a 401(k) plan because a professional money manager makes the difficult asset allocation decisions and market timing.

## Fixed-Income Managers

The fixed-income management style is more broad-based than the equity styles, because these managers can focus on a variety of factors. For example, some fixed-income managers focus on short-term maturities, whereas others focus on the longer term. Other managers move up and down the yield curve, depending on rates and projections.

Managers who move up and down the yield curve are trying to forecast interest rates and seek investment returns resulting from interest rate changes. For instance, such managers try to increase their exposure to long-term bonds when the managers expect interest rates to decrease. When the managers are correct, the long-term bonds that they hold increase in value, and the managers may sell them in order to realize a gain in the portfolio. Conversely, these managers will attempt to purchase short-term bonds when interest rates are expected to rise. If the managers are correct in this case, they are able to protect the portfolio from declining value. Further, the managers are able to repurchase at higher yields as the short-term bonds mature.

Although focusing on interest rates can be extremely successful, other fixed income managers believe that it is impossible to predict future interest rates. These managers buy bonds that have the same maturities but diversify the issuers between government and corporate. Historically, the spread between government and corporate bonds tends to broaden in difficult economic periods, while narrowing during good times.

Another fixed-income management style involves purchasing high-yield bonds that are below the investment grade level, commonly known as junk bonds. Although these investments can provide high yields, it is vital to communicate the downside, which is bond default risk to participants in 401(k) plans.

## GIC Managers

A GIC fund is a professionally managed, commingled pool of guaranteed interest contracts. GIC fund managers perform due diligence over the issuers of contracts, and then negotiate terms of the contracts. A good GIC manager will conduct rigorous evaluations of all issuers, rather than relying solely on insurance company ratings, to determine who will appear on the approved list. Normally, a well-diversified, pooled GIC fund will hold no more than 10 percent of the portfolio with any one issuer. Further, a well-managed GIC fund will consist of various maturity dates that range from one to five years.

Because these investments offer stability and yields comparable with intermediate-term bonds, a managed GIC fund is attractive as a conservative option for 401(k) plan participants. However, it is important to communicate to participants that although the intention of these investments is to maintain a stable value, there are no guarantee that participants will not lose money. Participants must understand that guarantee refers to the rate promised by the insurance company, and is not the same as the FDIC insurance. GICs are contended with extensively in Chapter 9.

# FOLLOWING INVESTMENT STYLE: "FUND DRIFT"

Once the sponsor has determined the management styles most appropriate for the employer's plan, it is imperative to find investment managers that follow their stated investment style. This concept, known as truth-in-labeling, refers to the idea that over time, funds should strictly follow their stated objective, as expected for funds of their type.

Unfortunately, not all mutual fund families line up. In theory, each mutual fund seeks to achieve a specific investment objective, and thus investors expect it to fall at a particular place on a spectrum of risk and reward. However, many funds do not fall on the spectrum where they are expected to be because of deviations in management style. These funds do not adhere strictly to their objectives year to year and thus increase the likelihood that they do not meet their objectives.

This overlap can have a negative impact on individuals who truly want to diversify their assets, and it can be a problem for plan sponsors trying to meet their fiduciary obligations. Clearly, plan sponsors cannot meet their obligations to offer funds with materially different objectives if the facts are different from the promises.

A range of funds that follows the concept of truth in labeling will reflect more predictable, consistent risk and reward over time. This type of consistent, historical performance could help participants choose funds with more predictably diverse investment styles and will provide the benefit of true asset allocation. The plan's consultant or financial advisor can conduct the kind of detailed style analysis necessary to address all fiduciary concerns.

# GATHERING BASIC INFORMATION ABOUT CANDIDATES

The search for investment managers should entail a rigorous interviewing and discovery process, during which the plan sponsors must learn certain vital information before making the final selection. Again, hiring a consultant or financial advisor to help with this process can prove most valuable to the plan sponsor because these individuals have such an in-depth understanding of management style, performance issues, and risk parameters.

The following list has been suggested for gathering information before conducting the actual provider interviews:

- History of the firm and background of key persons
- Minimum and maximum account sizes accepted, as well as total assets under management

- Breadth and depth of experience in portfolio management, research, marketing, trading, and operations
- Ownership of the company
- Investment philosophy and style(s)
- Structure of firm's decision-making process
- Source of research
- Credentials of key personnel
- Operational capabilities
- Fee[120]

## The Manager Interview Process

Once the plan sponsor has eliminated the inappropriate candidates, it is proper for investment managers to conduct a presentation. The presentation may focus solely on investment management services or on all aspects of the plan if the sponsor is seeking a bundled, full-service provider.

During the actual 401(k) service provider(s) (or investment manager(s)) presentation, plan sponsors should ask pointed questions with respect to the investment management of the plan. Try to get a sense for such factors as how investments are made; what investment philosophy or style the advisor uses; who establishes and/or monitors investment policy; and who determines what stocks, bonds, and so forth are purchased in a portfolio, and how. Ask questions about the key personnel's (especially the project manager's) credentials, background, and experience. Most importantly, understand the investment process that the manager will follow.

As with any selection process, there are certain pitfalls to avoid when a plan sponsor chooses an investment manager. Allowing corporate lending relationships to influence investment manager selection could pose some fiduciary risk. In addition, although past performance can provide some basis for investment manager evaluation, it should not be the sole reason for hiring a particular manager. Presentations of performance can vary dramatically in terms of time periods shown, comparisons to benchmarks, and so on, so plan sponsors should be cautious in terms of how much weight they give to investment performance in their selection process. Finally, the fees associated with investment management services deserve careful scrutiny during the selection process

---

120 DOL, Report on the Working Group on Guidance in Setting and Monitoring Service Providers (November 13, 1996).

simply because there are different fee disclosure requirements for the various types of investment management organizations. Fees are discussed in detail in requirements for the various types of investment management organizations. Fees are discussed in detail in Chapter 11.

## Performance Evaluation and Investment Style Monitoring

As part of their general fiduciary responsibilities under ERISA, plan sponsors must arrange for periodic evaluations of both the performance and management style for all investments in the plan. Failure to objectively monitor the plan's investment options could result in the loss of any protections under section 404(c) for participant-directed plans.

By setting parameters for and monitoring both investment performance and management style, plan sponsors can hold their investment managers accountable to certain standards. It is important to monitor style management in addition to performance because the truth in labeling issue discussed earlier. It is imperative for plan sponsors to monitor investment style to determine whether the manager's investment options are adhering to truth in labeling, and are, in fact offering varying risk and return characteristics. For example, if a plan offers a value equity fund option, which is described as pursuing both growth and income but actually invests in more volatile small-growth stocks to capture top performance, participants may be getting more volatility than that for which they bargained. In this case, the fund would not be following truth in labeling. Also, when a plan's investment options deviate from their stated investment management style, they may cause the total range of options to become too similar in their risk and return characteristics, which could jeopardize the plan's compliance with 404(c).

Therefore, investment option evaluations should include both a long-term performance review and performance attribution analysis, which will help detect any deviations in management style. As part of this review, plan sponsors should ask their investment managers to what factors they attribute a fund's performance, and they should question any deviations—good or bad— in the fund's performance and detect style deviation require a considerable level of analysis. Many plan sponsors may not feel equipped to conduct such analysis, in which case they should retain an advisor or consultant to assist them with the evaluation process and ultimately ensure the integrity of their investment option selections.

## Comparing Investment Performance

An important part of an advisor's role might be to help plan sponsors determine any benchmarks or indices that would be appropriate for monitoring investment performance. Some of the more common indices used for the equity or bond portions of a fund include the following:

- Standard and Poor's 500
- New York Stock Exchange Index
- Value Line Index
- Dow Jones Composite Index
- Wilshire Equity Style Index
- Lehman Brothers Government/Corporate Bond Index
- Morgan Stanley EAFE

The key to accurate tracking is to select an appropriate index with which to measure performance. In fact, no index is a truly perfect yardstick for measuring the performance of a given portfolio, because funds are managed with objectives that generally differ from the index. Moreover, the market indices have no associated transactional costs, which create a bias in their favor.

Nevertheless, the use of appropriate benchmarks can be useful in evaluating investment performance and detecting management style deviation. For example, a large-growth fund measured against a large growth index should show a correlation in performance explicitly. If one is up, the other should be up, and vice versa. If that same growth fund's performance moved in the opposite direction of the large growth index, this might indicate a deviation in management style; specifically, the fund manager might be buying something other than large growth stocks.

Another way to detect style deviation is to do a returns-based performance attribution, which compares portfolio returns to various style index returns and makes a judgment about the source of the performance. A large capitalization fund manager who attributes a significant part of performance to value stocks has clearly drifted from the stated investment style and should be held accountable.

## Calculating Rates of Return

Performance monitoring requires calculations of investment return. The rate of return is the percentage profit or gain achieved by holding an investment or portfolio for a particular time. In its most simple form, a rate of return is computed by subtracting the difference between the beginning and ending values and dividing this amount by the beginning value. The result is a decimal point return that can be converted to a percentage return by multiplying by 100.

For 401(k) plans, this simple calculation becomes more complex because of the inflows (contributions) and outflows (distributions) of cash from the portfolio. If either a contribution or distribution is made during the period measured with the equation, the calculation will break down. Thus, to calculate performance for 401(k) plan investment options, some other rate of return calculation is necessary.

### Time-Weighted versus Dollar-Weighted

There are two types of rate of return calculations designed to deal with inflows and outflows in a portfolio. The first is called a time-weighted rate of return, which is designed to eliminate the effects on the portfolio of the timing and magnitude of external cash flows. The other measure of return is called the dollar-weighted rate of return, which measures the impact of any inflows or outflows or assets. The time-weighted rate of return shows the value of one dollar invested in the portfolio for the entire period of measurement, whereas the dollar-weighted rate of return shows an average return of all the dollars invested in a portfolio for the measurement period. Generally seeking, the time-weighted rate of return is a more accurate measure of the investment manager's performance, because the manager does not have control over the timing of contributions and withdrawals in the 401(k) plan.

## SUMMARY

Over time, as fiduciary standards for participant-directed plans evolve, there will be more scrutiny of the investment selection process followed by 401(k) plan sponsors. To show that they engaged in disciplined investment selection and monitoring, plan sponsors must take measures to put a structured process in place. By creating an investment policy statement, not only will plan sponsors have a credible set of written standards, but also, more importantly, they will have a system in place to carry out their fiduciary responsibilities. Not only must plan sponsors carefully select investments for their participants, they must monitor performance and ensure both the suitability of the individual options and the overall integrity of the plan's investments.

# Chapter 9—MANAGING STABLE-VALUE INVESTMENTS IN THE 401(k) PLAN

As 401(k) plan assets grew during the 1980s, stable value investments, in particular guaranteed investment contracts (GICs) were among the most popular investment options for participant-directed defined contribution plans. In fact, stable-value investments represented over 60 percent of 401(k) plan assets during this time and as much as 80 percent of assets in some 401(k) plans. Estimates indicate that employees have directed roughly $300-to $400 billion into stable-value investments, including GICs, which speaks to the tremendous popularity of these vehicles among participants.

However, during the past two decades there has been a significant shift of 401(k) plan assets out of stable-value investments into a variety of other vehicles, so that probably less than 30 percent of 401(k) plan assets are in GICs. There are essentially three factors contributing to the decrease in stable-value investment assets. First, there have been several highly publicized credit problems among the insurance industry, and investors have learned that "guarantee" in GICs refers to backing of the contract by the issuer, not a government guarantee. More specifically, in the spring of 1991, Executive Life defaulted on its GIC obligations largely because of high exposure to low-quality (junk) bonds. Mutual Benefit Life followed suit just a few months later, suffering similar credit problems because of high exposure to commercial mortgages. Finally, Confederation Life posed the most recent credit problem, in 1994. Regulators to protect and maximize policyholder values seized all three insurance companies. The regulators acted quickly to provide assistance out of concern that these insurance companies would not be able to meet their obligations.

In the case of both Mutual Benefit Life and Confederation Life, the regulators were concerned about a run on the bank. Specifically, if the industry perceived that the company could not meet its obligations, everyone would turn in their chips and cause liquidity problems. The regulators wanted policyholders to realize that there was still considerable value left in these companies.

Second, the last two decades have seen plan sponsors offering a broader range of investment options. The difficulties experienced by these three insurance companies brought national attention to the issue of insurance company credit quality. These events were so significant that they altered the common view of GICs as virtually risk-free investments. Therefore, plan sponsors became concerned that perhaps participants might be misinterpreting the word guaranteed in GIC, and thus took measures to communicate more effectively about these products. With an improved communications effort, to clearly explain both the risk and reward of stable-value investing, participants gained a better understanding of these vehicles and recognized the importance of exploring additional options. Moreover, given that most plans have increased their range of investment options during the last decade, participants have taken advantage of their new choices, and diversified their assets out of GICs into equities and other types of options.

Third, improved communications have increased participant awareness concerning investment education and planning, which results in a better understanding of investment options. Although improved communications and more investment choices have provided participants with the necessary information to elect to shift some of their account balances out of GICs and create more appropriately diversified portfolios, clearly there is still a place for stable-value investments among their options. Despite recent events, as a stable, fixed-income asset category, stable-value investments offer plan participants a compelling investment story—virtually no volatility, modest credit risk, and stable, long-term return potential. Above all, it is important for both plan sponsors and participants to realize that the life insurance industry is fundamentally sound, and that generally financially strong institutions issue GICs. Compared to thrifts and banks, most insurers are better capitalized and generally possess better asset quality. Seriously troubled insurers have historically represented a small percentage of the universe. In addition, the introduction of newer alternative stable-value investments (discussed in more detail later) offers investors the opportunity to better diversify the risk of their stable asset portfolios.

# DEFINING STABLE-VALUE INVESTMENTS

Stable-value investments, the most common being GICs, are contracts issued by insurance companies or banks, offering a fixed rate of interest and a fixed maturity date. In general, no other investment option offers the combination of returns and stability that stable value investments provide. The issuer of the contract guarantees repayment of principal and accrued interest at maturity. Typically, the contract specified the terms, such as the date contributions must be made, and the actual timing and rate of interest and maturity payments. Additional terms ordinarily relate to benefit payments, penalties for premature termination, and other types of withdrawals. Returns on GICs are usually higher than rates on Treasury securities of the same maturities; however, a GIC is not a security and is not required to be registered with the SEC. They are governed by the Department of Labor.

Stable-value investments have a major advantage over other types of fixed-income investments, in that they are negotiated instruments, which mean that the terms can be modified to meet the specific needs of the plan. Another attractive feature of stable-value investments is that they are carried at book, rather than market, value. This means that they need not report a loss of principal if interest rates increase. In other works, plan sponsors can carry GICs at face value plus accrued interest. This fact has helped fuel their success in the marketplace.

In 1994, the American Institute of CPAs (AICPA) released a statement of position on the valuation of investment contracts in defined contribution plans. Essentially this statement confirmed the book-value treatment for GICs in defined-contribution plans, as long as the contracts are fully benefit-responsible. Contracts that are either partially or completely benefit nonresponsive must be reported at fair value. However, in 2004 the SEC had inquired into stable value investments. The SEC is questioning how the effect of low risk and higher returns than would normally be expected is produced. Specifically, they are perplexed how the wrap is valued. The wrap is the insurance agreements that allow the investment to maintain a certain net asset value. Sponsors should discuss this issue with their auditors to ensure appropriate accounting treatment. Figure 9-1 reflects the risk return comparison of stable-value investments to other assets classes.

## Figure 9-1

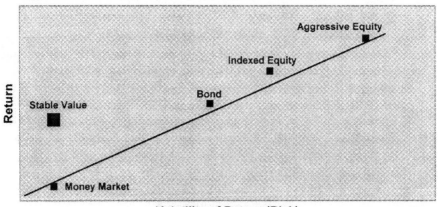

Risk and Return Comparing Stable Value to Other Asset Classes

There are several types of stable-value investments, designed to meet a variety of plan and participant needs. In addition, this marketplace has seen significant product development in response to investor demand. Among the types of stable-value investments available are the following:

- GIC—In a standard GIC, the assets are invested with an insurance company in a lump sum or in multiple deposits during a specified period (window), at the beginning of a contract, and remain invested for the duration of the contract, receiving a compounded interest rate. Most GIC contracts allow participant benefit payments and investment transfers at book value.

- BIC (Bank Investment Contract)—This investment contract is issued by a bank, rather than an insurance company, and the operation of a BIC is similar to the GIC. The bank issuing the contract guarantees repayment of principal and accrued interest at maturity.

- Window GICs—Window contracts permit periodic deposits during a specified time, usually three to six months. All deposits receive the guaranteed interest payment to maturity, generally three to five years. Because these contracts allow periodic deposits, they are sometimes attractive to 401(k) plans.

- **Immediate Participation Guarantees (IPGs)**—These contracts have interest rates that reset periodically (usually annually) and have no maturity date. Often no benefit withdrawals are permitted during a discontinuance payout period, which may present accounting problems because such restrictions cause the contract to not be fully benefit responsive.

- **Synthetic GICs**—These stable-value investments have experienced the most significant growth over the last few years. In fact, they have become so popular that they now comprise 50 percent or more of current placements, according to industry sources. Synthetic GICs consist of plan-owned fixed-income assets plus a book-value wrapper contract. The book-value wrapper is a contract between the plan and a financial institution allowing synthetic GIC contracts to be valued at their book value. The book-value wrapper contract issuer agrees to pay or advance employee-directed benefit withdrawals at book value, even if the market value of the fixed-income assets is less than book value.

In light of recent credit problems in the insurance industry, synthetic GICs have become enormously popular. In a worst-case scenario with a synthetic GIC, if the financial institution fails, the plan would only lose the book-value accounting. Said another way, the investment still has significant value because the plan actually owns the assets. The only action required by the plan sponsor in this case would be to purchase a new wrapper from a different financial institution.

Synthetic GICs, which offer either fixed-term or constant duration management, come in a variety of shapes and sizes. The simplest form is a buy and hold synthetic GIC, which consist of a single fixed-income security (such as an FNMA) that is owned by the plan, wrapped for benefit responsiveness, and is generally intended to be held until the security matures. With a synthetic GIC, the plan generally accepts the asset risk, whereas the company providing the wrap accepts the benefit responsiveness risk.

Synthetic GICs may have nonparticipating or participating wrap features. With a nonparticipating wrap, the issuer agrees to make up the difference between book and market value at the time of a benefit payment. Therefore, if at the time of a benefit payment the book value is higher than market value, the issuer makes up the difference, and if book value is lower than market value, the issuer retains the gain. As such, the asset performance experience resulting from withdrawal is borne by the issuer.

With a participating wrap, the impact of the gains and losses in market value are amortized over the remaining life of the contract through changes in the crediting rate. In this case, the plan retains the asset experience. The issuer still guarantees book value at the time of benefit payments, but then spreads the positive or negative effect over the remaining term of the contract. As a result, this type of wrap contract generally offers a lower fee than a nonparticipating contract, resulting in a higher net crediting rate on the synthetic GIC.

Next is the actively managed synthetic GIC, which consist of a portfolio of fixed-income assets that are owned by the plan, wrapped for benefit responsiveness, and actively managed by a fixed-income manager. The crediting rate is reset periodically (quarterly, semiannually, or annually), based on the investment experience of the portfolio. Essentially this is an actively managed fixed-income portfolio, where a manger makes buy and sell decisions; however, the wrap provides benefit responsiveness and the ability to use book valuation. The actively managed synthetic portfolio can be managed to either a targeted maturity date or a constant duration structure. Actively managed synthetic GICs are most appropriate for plans that have at least $100 million in assets (or that are able to commit at least $25 million to the synthetic strategy) in order to sufficiently diversify the portfolio.

Separate account GICs refer to a portfolio of fixed-income securities, held in an insurance company separate account, which have a book value wrapper provided by the same issuer. These differ from the actively managed GICs just discussed in that the investment management and the wrapper are both provided by the same insurance company. Recall that separate account assets are segregated from the company's general account, so that general account policyholders have no claim on assets held in the separate account. Separate-account GICs are book-value benefit-responsive contracts with variable rates based on the performance of a specific pool of assets that feature fixed maturities or constant-duration structures and a guarantee of principal by the issuer.

One significant trend in the development of stable-value investments is that most investment portfolios are now handled by intermediaries, including investment managers, advisors, and consultants, rather than directly by the plan sponsor. In addition, the added complexity of multi-party contracts provides even more reason for plan sponsors to hire a professional stable-value manager to evaluate and select appropriate stable-asset investments.

# INDIVIDUAL STABLE-VALUE MANAGEMENT VERSUS POOLED FUNDS

Usually a plan needs at least $50 million in GIC assets to access professional stable-value management on a separate account management basis. This amount is necessary so that the stable-value manager can properly diversify the portfolio among a number of holdings and products. As a practical matter, stable-value managers will try to diversify their holdings in a separate account so that any one issuer holds no more than 10 to 15 percent of the contracts in a portfolio. Further, the stable-value manager will attempt to spread the portfolio across contracts with a variety of maturities to spread investment risk and to ensure ongoing liquidity.

Smaller plans can access professional stable-value management through a managed stable-value pooled fund. In a pooled fund, each plan's stable-value assets are pooled with those of other plans, and the total amount is professionally managed. The size of the pooled fund allows the manager to properly diversify the portfolio, negotiate favorable terms for all participating plans, increase the yield on the portfolio, and invest in the most secure issuers; that is, offer smaller plans the benefit of larger individually is, offer smaller plans the benefit of larger individually managed portfolios. The benefits are low investment minimums, liquidity, and competitive returns. Still, one of the biggest advantages of a pooled fund for smaller plans is diversification and the ability to take advantage of new products, such as the growing synthetic market.

# STABLE-VALUE INVESTMENTS COMPARED TO OTHER ASSET CLASSES

Generally, stable-value investments compare favorably to money market investments such as money market mutual funds because of their longer duration. They also compare favorably to short-and intermediate-term bond funds, generally with less volatility.

To compare stable-value performance with that of other fixed-income investments, it is usually most appropriate to use a composite index comprising contracts of uniform denomination and maturity, but with structured purchase and maturity dates. One of the most popular GIC indices uses 60 five-year, $1 million contracts.

The primary reason for this performance is that GICs have virtually no volatility because they can be carried at book value. There is also a difference in total investment growth because of the slight yield premium that GICs typically offer compared to bonds.

Clearly, there is legitimate value to offering stable-value investments in a portfolio in combination with other assets. They are most appropriate for investors seeking stability of principal and/or those who have short investing time horizons. In fact, stable-value investments offer an effective fixed-income alternative to traditional stock/bond investment options in defined-contribution plans. They can reduce volatility on the fixed-income side and can serve as a core asset for the purposes of asset allocation. Perhaps now used more selectively by participants, the stable-value option is still very important among 401(k) investments; they have simply become a smaller piece of the pie.

# OPERATION OF INSURANCE COMPANIES

Before selecting GICs as investment options for 401(k) plans, it is useful to understand a little about how insurance companies operate with regard to revenues and investment portfolios. Large insurance companies can invest in several thousand different issues, from private placement bonds and mortgages to U.S. Treasury securities. In addition, they usually have tens of thousands of whole-life policyholders. Their portfolios tend to be well diversified and typically will provide a lot of revenue.

The revenues that insurance companies earn on their GIC holdings represent the difference between what the company is earning on its investment portfolio and what it is paying out on the GICs. Part of this revenue is used to offset administrative expenses, including marketing, and part of it builds reserves required by regulators. The balance goes to profit, which (in the form of retained earnings) strengthens the capital and surplus positions of the companies.

To understand the unique circumstances faced by insurance companies, compare them to manufacturing companies. If a large manufacturer never sold another product, its revenues would go to zero, it would go bankrupt, and eventually all inventory and assets would be sold to satisfy creditors. By comparison, if a large insurance company never sold another policy, interestingly enough, its profits would increase, because marketing expenses would be reduced. Existing policies would continue to generate income, and the company's investment portfolio would earn additional income. In essence, profits would rise.

The investment portfolio of the insurance company is important because it is one of the mainstays of any stable-value program. Typically, two-thirds to three-quarters of the portfolio is in investment-grade bonds, whereas 15 to 20 percent is normally invested in commercial mortgage investments. Although problem mortgages have made good fodder for the press, a look at the portfolios of most insurers reflects well-diversified portfolios characterized by small percentages of problem mortgages. Further, because there are several thousand bonds in the typical insurance company portfolio, it is normal to have one to three percent of bonds in default. Unfortunately, the focus of attention has been on a very small portion of large portfolios.

There are three kinds of risk associated with stable-value investments, including the risk of default, investment return risk, and interest rate risk. These terms are self-explanatory.

# MANAGING THE RISK OF STABLE-VALUE INVESTMENTS

Given the complexity of stable-value investments, plan sponsors are learning to rely on investment managers, either through a pooled stable-value fund or on a separate account basis, to manage their stable-value portfolios. Without such management expertise to back them up, plan fiduciaries are in the difficult position of being held to standards of expertise that few of them have.

In light of insurance company credit problems, credit analysis and expertise become paramount to the success of stable-value investments in 401(k) plans. As such, plan sponsors must seek external expertise in both the selection and ongoing evaluation of their GIC providers. A pure reliance on agency credit ratings is not enough from a fiduciary standpoint, given that some of these agencies had given now-defaulted GIC issuers their very highest ratings. Better still would be a careful and rigorous credit analysis tailored to the plan's investment policy standards, along with the use of synthetics to increase diversification.

# THE GIC MANAGEMENT PROCESS

Just as a 401(k) plan's other investment options require a careful selection and monitoring process, the same holds true for stable-value investments. In general, the process of managing a plan's stable-value investments should include the following steps:

- Develop mutually agreed-upon investment guidelines for stable-value investments, including credit and maturity parameters. These guidelines can be part of the plan's overall investment policy, as discussed in Chapter 8.

- Structure the portfolio by product types. Given the range of stable-value investments available, consider those with features that best suit the needs of the plan's participants.

- Set the asset allocation using traditional GIC contracts, buy-and-hold synthetics, and managed synthetics.

- Establish an appropriate maturity structure. Once more, consider the participant population's contribution and distribution patterns.

- Manage the portfolio in accordance with guidelines. As discussed earlier, using an intermediary or investment manager will provide the appropriate level of expertise to manage stable-value investments.

Add investments based on their relative value, considering the plan's diversification needs, spreads over treasuries, yield curve analysis, credit decisions, and sector analysis. Because product development, market conditions, and participant needs are constantly evolving, so too must the nature of the plan's stable-value investments. A consultant or advisor can help monitor the plan's stable-value investments and recommend changes as needed, or as market conditions warrant.

Throughout each phase of this management process, careful and rigorous credit analysis is crucial because:

- It is the best way to minimize credit risk.
- It facilitates greater issuer diversification.
- Relying solely on outside rating agencies is insufficient, according to recent surveys of the nation's top consulting firms.

## Phase I—Statistical Analysis

Statistical analysis of GIC issuers requires a through examination of each issuer in the areas of asset allocation, asset quality, reserves, capital and surplus, profitability, and liquidity. These data come from statutory reports, annual reports, investment schedules and reports, industry trade journals, pro forma financial statements, and actuarial simulation reports.

Although these data resources reflect a company's history, it is equally important to consider the company's future obligations for an individual plan's contracts as well as a multitude of others. Therefore, the statistical analysis must examine whether a company will be able to pay all of its obligations in the future. Additional analytical techniques include recession scenario testing (to see how the issuer would withstand a severe economic downturn) as well as capital adequacy testing.

This approach includes a forward-looking analysis of insurance company solvency called the recession scenario testing model. In this model, each insurance company is subjected to a stress test that assumes a severe economic downturn in all markets, leading to deterioration in the insurer's asset quality as well as a decline in operating earnings. This test starts with year-end numbers and extends out five years.

## Recession Test Assumptions

1. Earnings from operations for the next five years will be the average of the last five years, discounted by 50 percent.
2. There will be losses in the common stock portfolio of 20 percent the first year, 10 percent the second, five percent the third, and five percent the fourth.

3. Commercial mortgages will have a three percent annual foreclosure rate, with a 50 percent residual value.

4. Equity real estate will have doubled the nonperforming rate, with a 50 percent residual value.

5. High-yield bonds will have a 10 percent annual default rate, with a 40 percent residual value.

Only if an insurer passes this test, that is, proves that at the end of the five years there would still be sufficient capital and surplus to repay the funds invested in GICs, can it remain on the approved list. These conservative assumptions add an extra layer of protection for plan participants and for plan fiduciaries trying to fulfill their general prudence requirements.

## Phase II—Management Analysis

The goal of this second phase of this research is to make sure that any asset with a maturity of three to five years will be able to meet its obligation at the end of that period. It is necessary to review the fundamentals of a company by having conversations with insurance company management. Such conversations offer insights on how the management is dealing with current problems, if any, and on the company's general management philosophy. Interviews with senior management and investment officials of GIC issuers offer an opportunity to do the following:

- Ask questions arising from statistical analysis
- Understand investment strategies, underwriting guidelines, and operating procedures
- Evaluate problem assets, earnings estimates, profitability targets, target markets, and future products

## Phase III—Outside Research

The third phase of credit analysis uses the findings of rating services for comparison and reevaluation purposes, rather than relying on the ratings as a stand-alone resource. The dependability of rating agency data has been the subject of some controversy in the industry. For example, a new analyst at one rating agency downgraded a number of insurance companies in a rapid-fire succession. Unfortunately, rather than basing decisions on significant shifts in the insurance companies' fundamentals, the analyst seemed to be reacting to media hype on the alleged "impending death" of the insurance industry. Further, in the well-known Executive Life case, that company received the top rating of one of the public rating agencies right up until it announced the major write-downs in its portfolio.

Based on these examples, it is wise to thoroughly test the reliability of the rating agencies' methodologies and conclusions. In order to justify the acceptance of public credit ratings, two particular areas need intense research. First, determine the ability of the rating agencies to predict future claims paying ability of insurance companies. The use of public ratings for insurance companies is only justifiable if the agencies have some superior ability to predict future claims-paying ability. Second, if the rating agencies can predict future claims-paying ability, establish the time horizon for their predictions. In order for the data to be useful, the time horizon must extend beyond that of the investment in a GIC or insurance contract.

Despite the controversy surrounding them, the outside rating agencies do provide a reference point in beginning an issuer review. Thus, it is relevant to review their ratings, of only to confirm or contradict initial impressions. The independent rating services include the following:

- Standard and Poor's Corporation
- Moody's Investor Services
- Thomson Bank Watch
- Duff and Phelps
- The Townsend and Schupp Company
- A.M. Best Co

# COMMUNICATIONS FOR PLAN PARTICIPANTS

Participants benefit most from their 401(k) plan investments when they understand how each option works, and stable-value investments are no exception. Communicating to participants about stable-value investments requires special attention because of the misperception of the term guaranteed.

With such major emphasis on participants' education in particular providing them with sufficient information to make informed investment decisions as mandated by 404(c), plan sponsors can help limit fiduciary liability by exercising control with the use of the word guaranteed. In fact, many plan sponsors have decided to drop the word from fund names and descriptions altogether, choosing instead to call these investments the "stable-value fund," the "stable-asset fund," or the "stable-principal fund." The recent media attention to insurance industry credit problems presents a real opportunity for plan sponsors to refine and in some cases create more suitable stable-value communications materials.

In general, all stable-value communications pieces should cover the features and benefits of these investments, along with any risk factors. It is important, though, for participants to understand the measures taken to mitigate risk, such as thorough credit analysis and issuer selection criteria. More specifically, the most salient points for participant communications are as follows:

- **A description of the term "guaranteed"**
  Participants must understand that the federal government, any state government, the investment advisor, or the plan sponsor does not guarantee GICs. Instead, the guarantee refers only to the interest rate and maturity term of the contract. Because the safety of a GIC depends entirely on the strength of the issuer, plan sponsors should seriously consider dropping the word guaranteed in favor of stable-income or stable value.

- **Stable-value selection standards**
  Participants should receive information about the quality of the stable-value portfolio in which they have invested. They should also receive a summary of the minimum quality standards an issuer must satisfy in order to be included in the portfolio, along with the number of issuers, percentage limitations for any one issuer, and the average maturity of the contracts. In addition, similar information should be provided concerning the composition of GIC synthetics and the providers of wrap contracts.

- **Blended-rate accounting**
  Most plan sponsors use blended-rate accounting, which pools the interest on all contracts in the portfolio and credits it to participants' accounts based on their account balances. Unfortunately, blended-rate accounting does not allow for rate predictions or guarantees. The blended-rate changes constantly as deposits and withdrawals are made. Moreover, participant allocations are typically made based on trust earnings net of fees and expenses. To minimize confusion, plan sponsors should consider communicating actual return history and a recent fund yield, rather than a rate projection.

- **Benefit responsiveness**
  Benefit responsiveness refers to a stable-value investment's ability to pay out participant account balances at 100 percent on the dollar for all benefit events under the plan (death, disability, and retirement) regardless of market conditions. (Many other contracts provide an exception for so-called employer-initiated events such as layoffs and shutdowns.) Because payouts in these events may be subject to premature distribution penalties, participants should understand these conditions so there are no surprises.

- **Default provisions**
  Recent events have stirred participants' interest in what will happen to their stable-value investments if one of the issuers were to default. Sponsors should address this issue directly, describing any particular procedures they will follow, in the participant communications literature.

# NEW DEVELOPMENTS IN THE GIC ARENA

The explosive growth of synthetic GICs will continue, resulting in a range of new products in this area. The evolution of synthetics has recently included wrap contracts for troubled assets to allow them to maintain book valuation. In addition, structured-note GICs allow portfolio managers with a strong feeling on the future direction of interest rates to structure a contract whose rate may be tied to the performance of an external index. At the same time, the insurance company issuing the book-value wrapper takes on the exposure to fluctuation in market value.

A recent development in the area of participating and nonparticipating wraps is a sort of mix and match option, where the investor buys a combination of both. The issuer would underwrite a portion of the contract as participating and the remainder as nonparticipating. This combination results in the plan accepting the asset performance and withdrawal exposure for a certain percentage of the contract, after which the wrap provider assumes the exposure. This type of arrangement can result in a better contract rate than a purely nonparticipating contract, without taking on the exposure of a fully participating contract.

This market will continue to meet investor demand, particularly for products that adequately address the issue of credit risk. Although stable-value investments may not represent as large a percentage of 401(k) plan assets as they did several years ago, conceivably it was time for the much-needed scrutiny that resulted in new product development and appropriate use of these investment vehicles. Still very much a part of the 401(k) plan investment option pie, stable-value investments offer an attractive alternative for the conservative portion of a well-allocated retirement portfolio.

# Chapter 10—THE CHALLENGE OF PARTICIPANT COMMUNICATIONS

Recognized as one of the most important elements in 401(k) plan management, participant communications have received tremendous attention during the last few years. Participant communication is vital because, very simply, if participants are going to direct their own retirement investments, they must learn how to do it. Only effective participant communications programs will help them learn to make should investment decisions to improve their chances for financial security. In addition, it is up to plan sponsors and named fiduciaries to make sure their participants get this education.

Although the shift of investment control to participants and ERISA section 404(c) both mandate more attention to participant communications, plan sponsors genuinely feel a real sense of responsibility to give participants tools to plan for their retirement. As such, the commitment to participant communications is not just a matter of liability, but a genuine feeling on the part of the plan sponsor that it is the right thing to do. This sense of responsibility, along with growing media focus on the problem of inadequate retirement income, has driven the need to develop communications programs that go beyond minimum standards and legal requirements. Still, it is important to review the minimum communications standards under ERISA as the foundation of any participant communications program.

## MINIMUM COMMUNICATIONS STANDARDS UNDER ERISA

Except for the section 404(c) regulations and the communications requirements implicit within that section, ERISA contains few explicit participant communications requirements. Rather, as we will discuss later in the chapter, ERISA's participant communications standards as they relate to the fiduciary's responsibilities will continue to evolve under ERISA case law. These cases eventually will dictate minimum standards for participant communications.

## Summary Plan Descriptions

ERISA's statutory provisions require that participants receive a summary plan description (SPD), a booklet that describes the plan's provisions and the participants' rights and obligations in simple language. ERISA section 104(b) requires that each participant received an SPD no later than 90 days after first becoming a participant in the plan or within 120 days after the plan first becoming a participant in the plan or within 120 days after the plan first becomes subject to ERISA's reporting and disclosure requirements. For a new plan requiring IRS approval, the 120-day period begins the day after the IRS issues its approval. In the event that the plan is adopted retroactively, the 120-day period would run from the time the plan is adopted. Not only must plan participants receive the SPD, but also the U.S. Department of Labor (DOL) must receive one at the same time.

After the first SPD is provided to participants, the plan must provide an updated SPD every five years thereafter, including all plan amendments that have occurred within the five-year period. An SPD provides little in the way of usable information to plan participants, and most participants tend to ignore it. Rather, the SPD is a legally required communication that must contain certain information. Some plan sponsors use the SPD as a catalyst to describe all elements of the plan, transforming this otherwise-dry document into a viable communications piece. However, as a legally required communication, the SPD must contain the following information:

- Plan name
- Employer name and address
- Employer identification number (EIN)
- Type of plan (that is, defined contribution)
- Type of administration
- Name, address, and telephone number of the plan administrator
- Identity of designated agent for the service of legal process (and the address of such person)
- Eligibility requirements
- Statement describing joint or survivor benefits
- Statement and descriptions of vesting provisions
- Identification of trustee (including title and address)
- Statement of whether the plan is maintained pursuant to any collective bargaining agreements and when copies of those agreements may be obtained

- Statement of whether the plan is covered by termination insurance from the Pension Benefit Guaranty Corporation (not applicable in defined-contribution plans)
- The plan's fiscal year
- Sources of contributions and the methods used to calculate the amount of contributions
- Plan termination provisions
- Participant claim and remedy procedures
- Statement of ERISA rights of participants

The information that participants legally must receive is administrative and generally, concerns technical and operational elements of the plan, such as who the responsible parties are and how the participant should the responsible parties are and how the participant should seek remedy if his or her rights have been violated contrary to ERISA. Although this information is important, employees do not generally review SPDs because they are difficult to understand and do not seem to provide information that is relevant in the early enrollment stages of the plan.

The information contained in the SPD must be written in a manner that can be understood by the average plan participant. If there are a sufficient number of participants who have a first language other than English, they must receive with their SPD a written notice in that language to inform them of assistance available to help them understand the plan.

## Summary Description of Material Modification

In addition to the required initial SPD filing, any change in the plan that constitutes a "material modification" must be communicated to participants in a summary description of material modifications (SMM). The SMM must be provided to participants and the DOL within 210 days after the close of the plan year in which the material modification is adopted. In essence, a material modification is one that changes any of the information that was required to be included in the SPD.

## Summary Annual Report

The Summary Annual Report (SAR) provides participants and beneficiaries an annual statement summarizing the latest annual report (Form 5500). A SAR must be furnished on or before the last day of the ninth month following the close of a plan year in the same manner as applicable to the SPD.

## Participant Benefit Statements

ERISA section 105 requires that plan participants be able to obtain a benefit statement once per year. The industry standard for 401(k) plans is to provide quarterly participant benefit statements.

# RELATIONSHIP OF PARTICIPANT COMMUNICATIONS, FIDUCIARY RESPONSIBILITY, AND SECTION 404(c)

In addition to the legally mandated participant communications just discussed, there is an evolving standard for participant communications concerning the investment component of 401(k) plans. Participants need a certain amount of investment education in order to truly take control of the investments in there own accounts for purposes of section 404(c).

One of the objectives of giving participants control over their own investments is to allow plan fiduciaries to transfer the responsibility (and potential liability) for investment allocation from themselves to individual plan participants. Having control over their investments is a function of the participants' ability to invest in a broad selection of investment vehicles and make changes periodically. However, such control also requires that plan participants receive sufficient information about the plan's investment options to enable them to make informed decisions.

## Potential Liability

Under section 404(c), little protection is available if the fiduciary has not given participants sufficient information to enable them to make prudent investment decisions. As discussed in Chapter 7, these requirements provide both participants and the DOL an effective enforcement tool by which to impose liability on plan fiduciaries for imprudent investments. Rather than argue that the plan fiduciary was imprudent in his or her investment selection or monitoring, participants will simply argue that they did not receive sufficient information to make a prudent investment decision. As a result, the section 404(c) regulations put an enormous premium on participant communications.

This is a difficult, if not an impossible, standard. As described earlier, the section 404(c) protections require that in any given case where a plan fiduciary is claiming protection from a participant's own investment decisions, the fiduciary must show that the participant in fact exercised independent control over the investments in his or her account. In other words, it does not appear to be enough for plan participants to receive generic investment information about the investment options in the plan. Rather, it must be shown in each instance that the participant who is challenging the plan fiduciary actually was in control over the investments in his or her account. Whether this occurs depends on a number of elements:

- Whether the participant received the minimum required disclosures under the 404(c) regulation
- The sophistication of the participant
- The method in which the plan investments were communicated to the participant
- The ability for the participant to gain more information about the investments if needed

## Development of a Standard

As described earlier in Chapter 7, the section 404(c) regulations mandate minimum disclosure requirements for participant-directed plans. Although these requirements are significant, they are merely the beginning of a standard that will develop over time in the courts, just as all other fiduciary standards have evolved under ERISA. The reason these standards do not exist today is that participant-directed plans are still a relatively new development in the area of requirement plans. The DOL's regulations and future advisory opinions will provide a basis to which courts may turn in setting standards, but they will not be binding on the courts as definitive statements of law. As a result, the courts are likely to look at other areas of the law where the protection of individual investors' rights is paramount.

Because no minimum standards for adequate communications exist today, plan fiduciaries and their advisors should establish their own standards of prudence for participant communications. Plan fiduciaries need to consider the practical implications of ERISA's primary purpose to protect plan participants. In fact, both ERISA and section 404(c) were enacted to protect plan participants, not plan fiduciaries.

Accordingly, plan sponsors should approach participant communications from a standard of reasonableness. Applying common sense and taking into account all investment-related information made available to plan participants, the plan fiduciary should be comfortable that an average participant receives enough information to make a prudent investment decision. If this does not occur, the plan fiduciary must do more to inform and educate plan participants if the plan is going to continue to be safely as a participant-directed plan.

# INVESTMENT ADVICE VERSUS EDUCATION

Crossing the line between investment education and advice has been a major concern of 401(k) professionals trying to help plan participants make better investment decisions. In 1996, the U.S. Department of Labor (DOL) released its interpretive bulletin distinguishing between investment advice and investment information in participant-directed retirement plans.

With this interpretive bulletin, the DOL has tackled a particularly thorny issue for 401(k) professionals and plan sponsors that is, identifying at what point investment education would be considered investment advice.[121] This subtle distinction is critical. It allows people involved with 401(k) plan investment communications from inadvertently becoming plan fiduciaries and, as a result, engaging in prohibited transactions under ERISA. By defining precisely which types of information and materials would not be considered investment advice, the bulletin provides important safeguards for 401(k) professionals, who can now communicate to participants with certainty that they are not acting as fiduciaries. It also brings closure to a gaping hole in the regulatory structure governing participant-directed plans.

## Figure 10-1: The Line between Education and Advice

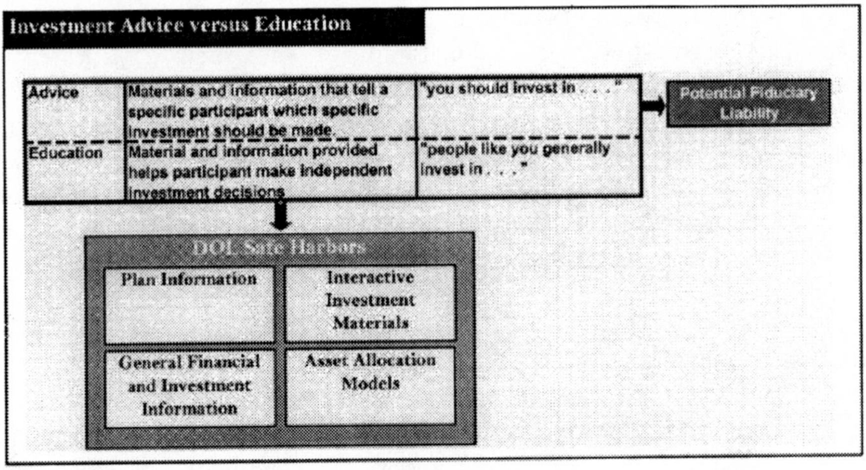

---

121 DOL, Interpretive Bulletin 96-1; Participant Investment Education; Final Rule (06/11/1996).

Both the DOL's approach to distinguishing investment advice from education and the historical factors that drove the need for such clarification will shape the future impact of this bulletin. First, the DOL clarified the applicability of ERISA section 3(21)(A)(ii), relating to the definition of a fiduciary under ERISA with respect to providing investment education materials. As noted in Chapter 7, a person is considered a fiduciary for a pension plan to the extend that he or she offer "investment advice" for a "fee or other compensation, direct or indirect."[122] Specifically, the regulations define as fiduciaries those people who, among other things, provide advice on a regular basis "pursuant to a mutual agreement or understanding"[123] that the advice will serve as the primary basis for a plan fiduciary's investment decisions.

The DOL's interpretive bulletin clarifies the scope of this fiduciary definition to include those people who provide investment advice to 401(k) participants. While 401(k) industry professionals have long recognized this regulation could be used to confer fiduciary status on people involved in plan communications, the lack of clear distinction between what constitutes advice has been an area of great concern. This is because much of the investment education information that is used in the 401(k) industry might be construed, under ERISA section 3(21), to be advice and that the people providing it could, in the absence of clear guidelines, be deemed fiduciaries.

Given the potential liabilities associated with fiduciary status, 401(k) professionals must know how far they can take education and still avoid this designation. Most 401(k) professionals do not want their activities construed as advisory for a number of reasons. First, if they were inadvertently deemed investment advisors by virtue of their education activities, 401(k) professionals would have to register as investment advisors with the SEC. In this regard, the SEC has indicated that employers who provide investment information of the type indicated in the DOL's interpretive bulletin would not be subject to registration or regulation under the Investment Advisers Act of 1940.[124]

---

122  ERISA §3(21)(A)(ii). The DOL has expressed the view that, for purposes of section 3(21)(A)(ii), such fees or other compensation need not come from the plan and should be deemed to include all fees or other compensation incident to the transaction in which the investment advise has been or will be rendered. See A.O. 83-60A (Nov. 21, 1983); Reich v. McManus, 883 F. Supp. 1144 (N.D. Ill. 1995).

123  See footnote 3 of Interpretive Bulletin 96-1 at 29 C.F.R. Section 2509.96-1.

124  DOL, Interpretive Bulletin 96-1; Participant Investment Education; Final Rule (06/11/1996).

Next, the communicator's education efforts might become prohibited transactions under ERISA section 406, if he or she is inadvertently deemed a fiduciary. As discussed earlier in Chapter 7, this section bars fiduciaries from engaging in certain transactions with a plan or its participants when there is a potential conflict of interest. The most obvious example in the 401(k) industry would occur where a mutual fund company is deemed to be providing advice to plan participants with respect to investments in that company's own funds. Generally, it would be considered a prohibited transaction for an entity to advise participants to invest in funds for which that entity or an affiliate earns management fees. As such, mutual fund service providers must take great care to ensure that their communications activities are purely educational rather than advisory in nature.

The fear of liability associated with participant communications has weighed heavily on the minds of plan sponsors and service providers for quite some time. Lacking a real definition of sufficient information, plan sponsors developed very real fears over potential litigation by participants who had poor investment performance in their retirement portfolio. As a result, most 401(k) professionals took the approach that more is better, even if they were not sure that their communications materials truly met the sufficient information requirement. Nevertheless, while 404(c) may have raised participant education to a higher priority level, it created greater concerns over liabilities associated with such aggressive participant education programs. No one really knew where to draw the line between investment education and advice, and thus avoid liability and fiduciary status. This is where the DOL finally stepped in.

Recognizing that absent clarification on this issue, professional communicators might limit their investment education programs, the DOL knew that more substantive standards were mandatory. Limited investment education was not an option given participants' general inability to make effective investment choices. As such, plan sponsors needed some structure to help drive their efforts to push participants up the investment learning curve.

The DOL's interpretive bulletin drawing a line between education and advice represents a long-awaited answer to the call for regulatory guidance on participant communications. Spurred by both the explosion in participant education programs and the confusion over 401(k), the DOL's bulletin offers much needed standards for those who want to create effective participant communications. Moreover, given the breadth in information that falls outside the definition of investment advice, the DOL's guidance will have a mostly positive impact on the business of participant communications.

## Taking Advantage of the Safe Harbors

The DOL's bulletin points out "safe harbors" or categories of information and materials that would not be considered investment advice.[125] These safe harbors include plan information, general financial and investment information, asset allocation models, and interactive investment models. Within each safe harbor, the DOL describes the characteristics of information and materials that would not be advisory in nature.

### Plan Information
Plan information may include the benefits of both plan participation and increasing plan contributions, the impact of preretirement withdrawals on retirement income, and the terms and operation of the plan. Descriptions of plan investment options, including their investment objectives, risk and return characteristics, historical return information, and prospectuses, are also included in this safe harbor.

### General Financial/Investment Information
Under this safe harbor, general investment concepts such as risk and return, diversification philosophy, dollar cost averaging, compounded return, and tax deferral are all considered appropriate. In addition, these communications may include historic differences in rates of return among asset classes; methods for estimating future retirement income needs; and ways to determine investment time horizons and risk tolerance.

### Asset Allocation Models
The fact that the DOL considers asset allocation models outside the realm of advisory is very good news for professional communicators. Considered one of the most effective ways to teach participants how to create their own retirement portfolios, asset allocation models have previously been considered close to the line of offering advice. Under this safe harbor, though, communicators may use models of asset allocation portfolios of hypothetical individuals with different time horizons and risk profiles, as long as the models are based on generally accepted investment theories and all material facts and assumptions are included. In addition, these models must include a statement that individuals should consider their other assets, in addition to their interest in the plan, when applying a particular asset allocation model to their own situations.

### Interactive Investment Materials
Another type of communication considered potentially advisory was interactive material that required input from the participants. However, allowing considerable

---

125. DOL, Interpretive Bulletin 96-1; Participant Investment Education; Final Rule (06/11/1996).

flexibility in its guidance, the DOL does not consider these communications advisory, as long as they adhere to certain standards. This safe harbor allows questionnaires, worksheets, software, and similar materials that give participants a way to estimate future retirement income needs and assess the impact of different asset allocations on retirement income. These materials must be based on generally accepted investment theories and should include all material facts.

In addition, there must be an objective correlation between asset allocations generated by the material and information and data supplied by a participant. Moreover, if the asset allocation generated by the materials identifies an investment option available under the plan, the materials must identify all other plan options with similar risk and return characteristics.

It is important to note that the safe harbors described above represent examples of the types of information and material that would not constitute investment advice when provided to plan participants. The DOL suggests careful consideration of the facts and circumstances involved in each element of an investment education program, to determine whether it would be considered advisory.

## The Bulletin's Affect on 401(k) Communications

Clearly given the breadth of information and materials that fall outside of investment advice, the DOL's guidance will have a mostly positive impact on participant communications and those involved in providing educational programs. The bulletin is an affirmation of what the best people in the industry have been doing to teach participants to make more appropriate investment decisions. Asset allocation models and interactive communications pieces have proven to be the most effective ways to influence participant investment behavior. Further, the DOL's guidance means a win for professional communicators, who will now have a clear understanding of what they can and cannot do without liability.

For large service providers, there will be little difficulty adhering to the DOL's standards, given that the types of materials and information contained in the safe harbors are common elements of their educational programs. As such, it will be simple for large service providers to structure their investment education programs to meet the criteria established by the DOL.

For brokers, financial advisors, and similar intermediaries, however, the DOL's guidance may require careful scrutiny and evaluation of their current educational activities. Because many of these individuals have placed themselves in advisory roles to participants, it is now very clear, according to the bulletin, which these people could be considered fiduciaries and, as a result, is subject to considerable restrictions.

# IDENTIFYING COMMUNICATIONS PROBLEMS

Although 404(c) certainly gives plan sponsors good reason to focus on effective participant communications, their own sense of responsibility to their employees also plays an important role. In any case, both factors should motivate plan sponsors to identify communications problems and take measures to resolve them.

Communication problems manifest most obviously when participants say that they do not understand the materials. In spite of this, plan sponsors should recognize several other symptoms of communication problem.

## Low participation

A common reason for lack of participation is failure to understand the plan. If the communications program fails to adequately explain the plan and its investment options to the employee population, eligible employees simply will not get involved. Further, if the communications program is not targeted to the appropriate levels (both investment sophistication and educational) for the employee population, it will also be ineffective and will result in low participation. The communications materials, much like advertisements, must target their message to the audience. If the employee population is relatively young and uninterested in saving for retirement, it is imperative to create communications materials that will appeal to this group.

Demographic issues such as a multicultural employee population may also influence the effectiveness of a communications campaign and result in low participation. If much of the employee population does not speak English, employees have little chance of understanding communications about the plan and therefore are not likely to participate. Plan sponsors with a multicultural workforce face additional communications challenges, which we will discuss later in the chapter, if they are going to increase the participation level of this type of employee population.

## Poor investment allocations

If a plan's participant population directs more than 50 percent of their assets into guaranteed investments and cash equivalents, undoubtedly there has been a failure to communicate the risk and reward characteristics of the other investment options as well as the importance of diversification. Participants who do not understand concepts such as inflation risk and the value of long-term investments in equities will often invest in the most conservative options simply by default or out of fear. Given effective communications about their investment options, participants can make appropriate decisions about allo-cating their retirement assets.

## Participant questions

One of the best ways to learn what participants find confusing or overwhelm-ing is to listen carefully to the kinds of questions they ask. The more general and infrequent the questions, the less participants truly understand about their 401(k) plan and their investment options. Participants who ask few ques-tions probably do not understand the plan enough to look for more details. In addition, if participants ask many questions about the same issue—for exam-ple, what is asset allocation—they can give plan sponsors clues about areas in need of further clarification and education. Service providers can be helpful to plan sponsors in identifying communications problems by sharing data from the telephone service lines. If telephone calls to representatives reflect regular occurrences of certain questions, perhaps about an investment option, the service provider can alert the plan sponsor to a possible need for better com-munication on this particular topic. Employee meetings also give the plan sponsor an opportunity to identify communications needs by listening to the types of questions asked during or after the presentation.

Although it is important to recognize communication problems, it is equally important to identify their case in order to determine and take appro-priate steps. Some of the most common causes of communication problems include the following:

## Participant communications lack stated objectives

A study on employee communications stated, "if an organization is to dissemi-nate information effectively about its benefit package to the employees, then these communication efforts must be mutually reinforcing and designed to achieve a specific goal."[126] In other words, the organization must use a strategic communication plan. Interestingly, this study concluded that most plan spon-sors do not develop their communications programs according to any written objectives, which is why many such programs fail. Without a set goal, commu-nications materials lack focus and often try to cover too many concepts in one piece, which results in information overload for the participants. As we will see later in this chapter, setting goals and objectives for the communications pro-gram is paramount to its success and ultimate benefit to the participants.

---

126 Michael C. Giallourakis and G. Stephen Taylor, "An Evaluation of Benefit Communication Strategy".

## Participant communications are treated as a one-time event or campaign

Much like an advertising campaign that assumes people will only change their behavior after absorbing the same message several times, a communications program must deliver messages to participants on a regular, ongoing basis. The program should be a process, rather than an event, to give participants the opportunity to absorb the material in stages, and have the chance to ask questions along the way. Treating communications, as a single event that occurs early in the introduction of the plan results in participants not fully understand their plan; therefore, they may choose not to participate. Only an ongoing process rather than a one-time event will help participants become educated investors who can make prudent decisions about directing their retirement savings plans.

## Participant communications are too generic

When communications are too broad and generic, participants do not absorb the concepts because the material does not feel relevant to their particular situation. Whether the communications medium is print, slides, or video, employees simply do not related well to generic examples. Instead, eligible employees need to see how participation will influence their own situation. For example, participants need to understand how much it will cost them in real dollars out of their take-home pay to participate in the plan at different contribution levels. They should also be aware of how much their employer will match their contributions so that they can see the direct impact on their own saving levels. The tone and content of communications must be appropriate for the employee population or employees will not pay much attention to a highly sophisticated discussion of investment concepts.

Service providers have recognized the need for customized participant communications and have responded by producing innovative communications programs that can be tailored to individual plan specifics. Many service providers have created modular communications materials that enable plan sponsors to select certain kinds of material and create a customized program for their participants. Modular communications materials come in all sorts of media including print, video, and slide presentations. Plan sponsors can choose modules that focus on basic investment concepts, plan provisions, or the benefits of tax-savings associated with participating in a 401(k) plan. The point is that service providers have created a way for plan sponsors to tailor their communications program to meet the needs of their specific employee population.

Many of the communications materials offered by service providers can be customized with the plan sponsor's logo, which often makes the plan feel more familiar to the participants. Furthermore, service providers should consider employee demographics, such as educational levels and ethnicity to create effective materials that present concepts either graphically or in alternative languages. There is a significant trend toward customization of participant communications simply because more targeted materials can have a greater impact on participation.

## Too much emphasis on print materials

The most commonly used medium for participant communications is still print, but the most effective programs use a multimedia approach instead. Employees do not like to read written employee benefit communications because the concepts can be complex, and print materials are a one-way communication that do not allow for questions and answers. In addition, a recent study noted that more than 27 million U.S. employees are functionally illiterate, so plan sponsors must use other media to communicate plan details to participants. Colorful graphics, posters, and attention-getting devices used to get employees interested in the plan can often be much more effective in raising participation levels than can printed materials.

A multimedia approach not only gives participants several opportunities to digest information about their plan but also offers plan sponsors a chance to encourage participants to learn more. Further, the multimedia approach is essential for an organization that has a multicultural workforce. This type of employee population may not absorb printed plan information because of a language barrier, so plan sponsors must present plan details and investment concepts in some visual manner that enables their employees to understand the plan and have the opportunity to ask questions. Studies have shown that some media are more effective for communicating a message to the various ethnic groups. For example, certain cultures might respond better to oral communication than to printed materials. Others may be more oriented toward saving, so communications efforts must be tailored accordingly.

Assessing the cause of communications problems will help sponsors develop better programs. Very simply, communications programs must be evaluated on a regular basis and modified accordingly. Using participant surveys, reviewing telephone inquiries, or soliciting some other type of participant feedback, plan sponsors can evaluate the impact of the communications program and determine the topics on which participants need further education.

# PARTICIPANT NEEDS

One of the best ways to head off communications problems before they occur is to truly understand what participants need in terms of education and information about their 401(k) plan. By doing some front-end analysis of the employee population, including demographics and investment sophistication levels, plan sponsors can get a good sense of how to construct a communications program that will have the greatest value for their employees.

As a rule of thumb, participants need real guidance and considerable hand-holding as they take control of their retirement investments. The trouble is that most plan sponsors are wary of providing this level of assistance because of fiduciary concerns—they cannot be seen as giving advice. Section 404(c) and its corresponding regulations attempt to absolved plan fiduciaries of any responsibility for participants' own investment allocations under certain conditions. Moreover, a fiduciary has no obligation to advise participants specifically with respect to their investments in a participant-directed plan, nor should this occur. Fortunately, as discussed earlier in this chapter, the DOL has clarified the distinction between information and advice so plan sponsors can avoid inadvertently crossing this line.

Yet many plan sponsors now offer their participants access to outside financial advisors to help them put their total financial picture in context in addition to determining suitable investments for their 401(k) plans. From a liability management perspective, plan sponsor concerns have changed significantly, following the shift of investment control to participants. Whereas plan sponsors were once concerned with the risk of giving bad advice concerning the investment of participant's retirement plan assets, now they must contend with the risk of not providing enough guidance. Plan sponsors now fear that participants who encounter pool investment performance in their 401(k) plan accounts could take action against their employers for not giving them enough information to invest wisely. As discussed earlier, the courts will determine the standards for this type of action.

So the challenge for plan sponsors is to create a communications program that provides enough guidance for participants to comfortably direct their own 401(k) plan investments, without crossing the line of providing advice—no small task. The real key is to help participants learn that they feel comfortable making choices on their own. An effective communications program will provide the tools for participants to become educated investors, rather than apprehensive savers.

# The Needs of a Multicultural Workforce

One of the toughest parts of making sure employees have the tools and information to make sound investment decisions is dealing with a multicultural workforce. For ethnically diverse employees, simply providing information is not enough; plan sponsors must ensure that these employees actually understand the materials. Fortunately, there are practical solutions for communicating investment information to a multicultural workforce. Recognizing the growth of multicultural employee populations and their clients' need for effective communications, a few leading companies provide a variety of services such as multilingual investment education materials, prospectuses, and enrollment meetings. In addition, desktop publishing systems allow plan sponsors to produce multilingual versions of employee newsletters without adding significant cost or resources.

Although removing the language barrier may help the communications effort, diversity experts caution plan sponsors to be sensitive to dialects, such as Mexican Spanish versus Puerto Rican Spanish, and to be sensitive to the educational levels of the participants. Too often organizations assume their employees have a much lower educational level than is actually the case, simply because they do not understand English.

Choice of medium also plays a critical role in communicating effectively with a multicultural workforce. By using posters to capture ideas simply and videos with colorful graphic presentations, plan sponsors can deliver one message that will reach several cultures. Communications experts also suggest that multilingual enrollment meetings improve the level of understanding because they give participants a chance to ask questions and receive answers in their native language. Multilingual enrollment meetings also give plan sponsors an opportunity to assess their participants' level of understanding and to get a sense of where they might need further education.

# Designing an Effective Communications Campaign

Designing a communications campaign should be much like building a house. It requires careful planning, a detailed schedule, and an assembly of key players (communications professionals) who will be involved in the process. Most importantly, an effective communications program must have goals and objectives set before construction begins.

It helps to think of a communications program as having three major elements: The message, the method, and the medium. First, the message refers simply to whatever points sponsors want to get across to the participants.

Items to consider are what the sponsor want participants to learn or gain from a communications program or what the participant should take away from the message communication. Next is the method, which refers to the manner in which the program will be constructed, including one-time communications (enrollment meetings) and ongoing elements (newsletters and quarterly statements). Finally, there is the medium, or how these messages will be communicated with the employees, whether it is in print, audio, video, or another format such as the Internet. More often than not, the communications medium will be a combination of these methods.

Before each of these elements is discussed in more detail, it is important to review the necessity of assembling resources and setting a schedule for a communications program. The determination of who will actually create and implement the communications program must be resolved. In keeping with the general trend toward outsourcing, many plan administration functions, most plan sponsors seek outside assistance for their communications programs. The larger service providers usually offer a comprehensive communications program as part of their bundled service package. These programs include various elements such as printed brochures, enrollment meeting slide presentations, videos, posters, streaming video, web applications, and a variety of ongoing communications materials.

Some of these elements may be standard, off-the-shelf pieces, but most contain good, basic information about 401(k) plans in general as well as important investment concepts. In addition, many service providers offer custom communications programs, in which they will tailor materials to the plan sponsor's employee population, plan provisions, and specific investment options. Custom communications campaigns are most effective because they take a targeted approach toward educating the plan sponsor's employees, taking into account demographics, investment sophistication levels, and general corporate culture.

Plan sponsors seeking a custom communications approach for a smaller plan can take advantage of the expertise of a financial advisor associated with their 401(k) plan. Uniquely qualified to educate individuals about investing, some advisors spend much of their time distilling difficult investment concepts down to layperson's terms. Further, a financial advisor who is working directly on other plan administration issues will be familiar with the employee population, plan provisions, and any particular challenges the plan faces, so that he or she can offer extremely valuable assistance in participant communications.

Clearly, plan sponsors gain access to valuable resources and expertise by outsourcing their communications programs, given that both large service providers and financial advisors understand participants' educational needs. In many cases, plan sponsors simply lack the expertise necessary to determine what is sufficient investment information for participants and how to present it most effectively. By taking advantage of external resources for communications programs, plan sponsors can make sure that they will meet their participants' educational needs and fulfill their fiduciary responsibilities.

Once plan sponsors have assembled key players and determined the resources for their communications program, implementers must develop a detailed, realistic schedule to implement the program. It is important to consider major plan milestones in putting together a schedule for the communications program. For example, if plan sponsors are switching service providers, they must build their communications program around milestones such as when plan assets move to the new provider, when new telephone and Internet services become available, and when participants can start switching among new investment options. These events will influence a communications program schedule because it is vitally important to let participants know when each milestone occurs and what steps they need to take with their own plan accounts.

Keeping participants informed and educated before any major plan events take place is essential to maintaining the integrity and credibility of the plan. The more up-front understanding participants have of their plan's provisions and operations, the more likely they are to take advantage of its benefits. Participants are more likely to understand these benefits if the communications program takes into account the three elements discussed previously: the message, method, and medium.

## The Message

Determining the message to communicate is much the same as setting the goals and objectives of the communications program. The question of the motivating need to communicate must be addressed. In other words, an assessment of what are participants should gain from the program. Not all communications programs set out to achieve the same goals and having a clear understanding of the motivation or issue behind the need to communicate helps create an effective message. For example, some programs are designed to introduce a new 401(k) plan, in which case they will focus heavily on messages about plan benefits, tax savings, and the need to plan for retirement. On the other hand, a communications program geared toward increasing diversification might contain more messages about the advantages of investing in stocks, taking a long-term approach, inflation risk, and the benefits of asset allocation.

Although each plan and employee population has different communications needs, there are some basic messages that should be part of every communications program:

**Why save?**—Explaining the need to start preparing for retirement early is one of the most critical messages in a communications program, because it motivates employees to participate in the plan. Media coverage of the United States' savings crisis along with concerns about reaching retirement without enough money to live on should be strong motivators for employees to take advantage of their retirement savings plan. In addition, disappearing Social Security benefits, longer life expectancies, and the rising cost of living are key messages for employees who do not pay enough attention to their retirement needs. Though these messages may sound like fear tactics, they have proven to have significant impact in helping employees understand the consequences of not saving for retirement. From a liability and simple responsibility standpoint, plan sponsors who have consistently communicated these messages can take comfort in the fact that they have made an effort to help their employees provide for a more secure future.

**The benefits of a 401(k) plan**—Once motivated, employees need to understand how to use the tools available to them, one of the most valuable being their 401(k) plan. From the beginning, the communications program should stress the benefits of participating in a 401(k) plan: tax savings, a convenient and disciplined savings plan that helps them save before they spend through salary reduction, and the possibility of extra savings through employer matching contributions. It is important for participants to realize that by using a tax-advantage retirement savings plan, they are actually keeping more money in their own pocket and thus can truly afford to save some money despite the fact that they may have a limited budget.

Introducing participants to the concept of tax-deferred earnings and the power of compounding can also help motivate them to participate in their 401(k) plan. This concept helps people recognize the potential to build up more money in their 401(k) plan than they could with a regular taxable savings account.

**Selecting investments/asset allocation**–Every communications program should include basic investment education so that employees understand how to choose the most suitable investments for their individual needs. Most employees are unsophisticated investors who feel so overwhelmed by industry jargon and information overload that they simply choose the most conservative investments by default. Investment education does not have to be complicated and should target the lowest sophistication level, while maintaining the interest level of those who may be more financially discerning. Well-educated people do not necessarily know a lot about the fundamentals of investing. The entire employee population should have access to basic investment information, including a discussion of the various asset classes, risk and reward characteristics of each type of investment, risk tolerance and time horizon considerations, and the value of taking a long-term approach to investing for retirement.

Effective communications help employees understand risk and their own tolerance for it. Participants must learn about the different types of risk associated with investing and how they feel about taking risk. The should also be asked to consider their time horizons for investing, which is one of the most critical factors in helping them decide on their own asset allocation. Many participants do not understand the concept of investing for the long term and that if they have several years until retirement, they should probably consider some investments in equities.

Only by seeing the advantages of investing more aggressively and diversifying their 401(k) plan investments will participants actually change their behavior and choose investments that are more suitable. Part of this motivation should come from communicating clearly the difference between taking market and investment risk versus inflation risk. Once participants realize that by investing too conservatively, their savings will not grow fast enough to keep up with inflation, they usually have more incentive to allocate their assets accordingly.

## The Method

Although this may seem like a lot of information for employees to absorb, the method of delivery is just as important as the messages in a communications program. Some of these messages are more appropriate in an up-front, more elaborate presentation, such as an employee meeting, whereas others are best delivered on an ongoing basis. Educating an employee population should take into account the fact that employees do not necessarily absorb the message the first time they hear it, and in some cases, they must receive it several times before they truly understand and can act on the information. In addition, using ongoing communications to supplement employees' initial introduction to the plan, its benefits, and options avoids overwhelming employees with so much information that they simply tune out and do nothing.

Ongoing communications are suitable for reinforcing certain investment concepts such as the need to invest for the long-term rather than reacting to short-term vicissitudes in the market, as well as for delivering performance information. In fact, participants should receive performance information at least on a quarterly basis, preferably with their statements. Providing a summary of market conditions with the performance data helps participants understand why their investments performed in a certain manner, because the market data sets a context for the performance figures.

Access to a toll-free telephone number for customer service is considered an ongoing communication, because employees can speak with well-trained representatives who can discuss investment option suitability. For other ongoing communications, it makes sense to schedule and deliver materials in whatever way has the biggest impact on participants. For example, if a plan intends to add new investment options within the next three to six months, it might make sense to use a statement stuffer or back slip in the participants' quarterly statements, describing the new investment options soon to be available.

## The Medium

The medium used for participant communications can have a huge impact on the program's effectiveness. Communications professionals agree that the most successful communications programs take a multimedia approach, using a variety of media to deliver different messages. Participants are typically busy people who are bombarded with hundreds of messages a day, so plan sponsors must creatively use different media to focus their participants' attention on the plan. Several service providers who understand the importance of participant communications have devoted substantial effort and resources toward making multimedia communications programs available to plan sponsors, including print, video, audio, and computer software.

For the initial introduction to the plan, employee meetings with either slides or laptop computer presentations are most effective because they allow the presenter to tailor the meetings to the audience. In most cases, these enrollment meetings can be customized to reflect a particular plan's provisions and investment options. During the course of the meeting, employees have the opportunity to ask questions, which not only help them better understand the material, but helps the plan's sponsor see areas of education that might need further attention.

Enrollment meeting presentations, whether by slide or video, are usually supplemented by print materials, so that employees have another resource to refer to either during or after the presentation. By using both media, the presentation is more effective because it is not necessary to pack all of the details into the video, which can make it overwhelming and less interesting. Another way to make the greatest use of an enrollment meeting is to send employees printed plan information beforehand. This way, employees have a chance to review the material so that the concepts presented during the meeting will not seem as foreign.

Meetings are also an effective medium for reenrollment, to introduce investment options, or to communicate any other major plan changes. It is a good idea to consider reenrollment if any of the following events have occurred:

- Significant levels of new hires
- Merger or acquisition of a new division
- Significant numbers of newly eligible employees
- Unusual reductions in plan participation percentages
- Changes in ownership of the plan sponsor

During the communications planning stages, some plan sponsors decide that whenever plan participation drops below a specified percentage, such as 75 percent, they will do a reenrollment communications campaign. This is a good way to focus on a major communications effort on a regular basis.

In terms of other ongoing communications, some elements of the program are best delivered through attention-grabbing devices such as posters, tabletop displays, or bulletin boards. Using colorful graphics and short, punchy messages, these media can direct employees' attention to upcoming meetings about the plan, new investment options, or ways to get more information. Finally, information like performance figures is usually best delivered through print media such as quarterly statement stuffers, employee newsletters, or performance highlight sheets, which allow employees to take the time to understand the figures.

The key to selecting the most effective media is to consider what will have the greatest impact on an employee population. If employees are likely to read a benefits newsletter, then that might be one of the best ways to communicate with them. Alternatively, if they gather around bulletin boards in hallways, this might be a good place for an attention-getting message about the plan. The point is to consider employee behavior during selection of media for a participant communications program.

Of course, certain media are effective with one employee population but not others. Computer software to assist in retirement investment planning can be highly effective for employees who are comfortable learning in this manner. These programs, available from large service providers, take the employee through a systematic process of figuring out how much money they need to save to maintain a certain standard of living during retirement, and what investments might be most appropriate to help them achieve their goals.

Innovative technology provide a means for plan sponsors and service providers to achieve one of their most critical goals with respect to participant communications—on-demand information. As participants become more accustomed to directing their retirement investments, they will need more education and information resources to manage their accounts effectively. Additionally, in keeping with a trend toward total benefits outsourcing, eventually participant communications will encompass all employee benefit information. The goal is for participants to use one resource to get all of their benefits information. Therefore, although sufficient information has been top priority for participant communications over the past few years, "integrated information" will be the buzzwords, and the challenge through this century.

# Chapter 11—SELECTING THE 401(k) SERVICE PROVIDER

After reading the first ten chapters of this book, there should be a good sense of the issues to consider before beginning a search for a 401(k) service provider. It helps to envision the 401(k) process as having three components: planning, implementation, and ongoing operations. First, planning includes plan feature selection, investment approach, and communications planning. Next, implementation includes fund selection, participant education, and plan installation. Finally, ongoing operations comprise participant services, record keeping, and measuring quality standards. The bottom line is that employers will need to rely on the support of their service provider and consultant or financial advisor for each part of the overall 401(k) process.

The enormous popularity of 401(k) plans has increased the complexity of service provider selection, simply because there are so many more choices today than there were a few years ago. Therefore, the selection process should involve careful research, analysis and most importantly, the assistance of outside experts because the success of a 401(k) plan depends heavily on the service provider. No matter how large or small a company, and regardless of the business, a 401(k) service provider selection process should begin with a careful assessment of a plan's individual needs. By looking first at the plan, an employer will know what to look for in a service provider, and narrow down the field based on a plan's requirements.

## ASSESSING A PLAN'S NEEDS

Although a plan may have some unique issues, certain baseline products and services are essential to the operation of any plan, and employers should expect them from a service provider. These baseline elements include the following:

- A broad range of diverse investment options
- Several prototype plan documents that are preapproved by the IRS
- A toll-free telephone service line and robust Internet access allowing participants access to account information and service

- A record-keeping system offering flexibility in account valuation and transaction processing
- Daily processing of plan and participant transactions
- Daily valuation of plan investment options
- Comprehensive reporting, including quarterly participant statements
- Assistance with group enrollment meetings and the enrollment process
- Participant communications/education support
- Fiduciary support
- Compliance capacities

Beyond these baseline services are an abundance of additional items that might be important to a plan. Trustee services, extensive voice response transaction capabilities, custom communications, and customized reporting are among the more common extras that may weight heavily in the selection process. For a straightforward plan, however, a service provider must offer, at a minimum, the services just listed. It is essential that during the planning phase the plan sponsor addresses its additional service needs. One valuable source of input is employee feedback. That is, to explore what employees are asking for with respect to their retirement plan. Remember that the 401(k) plan is an employee benefit, and the best way to make it more valuable to employees is to make sure it meets their needs. For example, if employees ask for a more diverse range of investment options, employers may want to look at service providers who offer a broad range of choices. On the other hand, if employees have anything but a nine-to-five work shift and need account access around the clock, a service provider with a twenty-four-hour voice response phone service is advantageous.

Once an employer has a good sense of a plan's needs, they must determine the best place to obtain these services, based on the size of the plan. A plan's size, in terms of both assets and number of participants, will dictate the most cost-effective way to service the plan. In most cases, using a bundled service package provides certain economies not available through an unbundled service arrangement.

# THE ROLE OF A CONSULTANT/FINANCIAL ADVISOR

Regardless of a plan's size and service requirements, using a consultant or financial advisor can maximize the efficiency and ultimate success of the service provider selection process. By engaging a qualified third party who provides information necessary for appropriate choices, plan sponsors can address fiduciary liability concerns. And, given the complexity of the 401(k) plan service business, a consultant or financial advisor is essential to help plan sponsors sift through the abundance of services available and help them make the best decisions.

The expertise of a consultant or financial advisor will result in a more meaningful search, as these individuals are familiar with the broad array of services available. The consultant or advisor should start by working with the employer to identify the company's particular needs and requirements. Not only is a consultant or advisor well informed about the market in general, but also he or she can take the time to understand the plan's goals and requirements, and then find appropriate service provider that match those needs. Further, the service providers' decision no longer rests with one individual in a company; instead, the decision requires input from areas such as treasury, benefits, and legal, each of who has unique requirements for the service provider. As such, an intermediary is critical to managing and streamlining the selection process by understanding the concerns and communicating with each of the decision makers. Very simply, given the complexity of plan management and the number of available service providers, the selection process would be unmanageable without the expertise of a consultant or financial advisor.

How an employer uses the consultant or financial advisor depends entirely on the plan's size and budget. For some plans, the advisor's role is actually part of the communications and employee education function. In other cases the consultant may be used exclusively to help sponsors select and monitor service providers, and to undertake required periodic investment manager performance analysis.

The point is that consultants and financial advisors may act in different capacities, depending on what suits a plan. In any event, the consultant or advisor selected should specialize in 401(k) plans, not just any CPA, stockbroker, or attorney, and bring several years of similar experience to the management of a plan. Finally, it is important that the consultant or advisor be familiar with several service providers rather than maintain an affiliation with just one, so that he or she can be independent, and help select the best provider for a plan.

# NARROWING DOWN THE FIELD

Before conducting a thorough review of any one service provider, it is useful to survey the market in general. Having a sense of what types of services are available and how they are delivered will not only educate plan sponsors about their own plan needs but also help narrow down the field of available providers. The employer may be familiar with both request for information (RFI) and request for proposal (RFP) to assist in the selection process. A consultant can assist in this matter. In most cases, it is best to start with an RFI because it involves a less cumbersome process than the RFP, and gives a good overviews of what a service provider can offer. Essentially the RFI helps plan sponsors give directions to their consultant in developing the RFP. The RFI helps plan sponsors become knowledgeable buyer s so that the most value from the selection process that follows.

When reviewing the information from service provider candidates, recall the most important issues from the previous chapters.

## Investment Management

A 401(k) plan should have a broad range of investment options with diverse risk and reward characteristics. The range of investment options should enable participants to create asset allocation strategies suited to their risk tolerance and investment time horizons. Included among the options should be conservative choices, such as stable value, fixed-income, balanced, equity, and aggressive growth to provide the full spectrum of risk and reward characteristics.

These investments should stay true to their investment style, that is, follow the objectives and policies stated in the prospectus so that they fall along the risk/reward spectrum as would be expected. This concept, called truth in labeling, is important because it results in consistent historical performance that helps participants choose funds with more predictably diverse investment styles. Further, truth in labeling ensures that a plan's investment options will provide the benefit of asset allocation and address fiduciary concerns with respect to suitability of investment choices.

All plan sponsors should develop guidelines for selection and monitoring of their plan's investment options, in the form of an investment policy statement. The statement should also contain parameters for investment performance and methods by which to measure that performance. Again, a consultant or investment advisor can assist the plan sponsor in these efforts.

## Participant and Plan Sponsor Services

Participants should be able to access account information and make transactions on a daily basis. Toll-free telephone services with both live representatives and voice response system capabilities should be available to participants; and in more recent times, account access through the Internet.

Participants should receive accurate account statements at least on a quarterly basis.

Record-keeping technology should minimize the administrative burden of plan sponsors and should accommodate specific plan provisions. The service provider should demonstrate a true commitment to bringing the most innovative technology:

- Electronic interfaces that ensure speed, accuracy, and quality
- Image processing for storage, retrieval, and document tracking
- Automated work distribution
- Optical character recognition
- Artificial intelligence software, checking systems, and so on
- Call routing and caller identification to route calls to a customer service representative who has immediate access to all relevant information
- Both regular and ad-hoc reporting should be available for plan sponsors, for both participant and plan-level data
- Single-source bundled service arrangements are generally more desirable because of cost efficiencies, smoother interactions among plan function areas due to electronic links, and generally one point of contact

## Participant Communications

Because participant communications are one of the most powerful ways to change investor behavior, sponsors need a service provider that has both experience and demonstrated success with participant communications programs.

Participant communication/education must be approached as an ongoing process rather than an occasional event. The communications should include three phases:

1. Communicating to employees about the new plan.
2. Educating employees about evaluating their choices and allocating their assets during enrollment. A financial advisor can serve as an excellent resource for this education process.

3. Providing ongoing communications to keep participants up-to-date on fund performance and retirement investment strategies.

Participants learn about investing concepts in stages and must receive information in pieces rather than being subjected to information overload. Therefore, the service provider should offer an integrated, education program designed to increase participation, raise contribution levels, and improve asset allocation at different stages in the participants' education process.

The participant communications program should be tailored to the specific employee population. Employees vary in their levels of investment sophistication, general educational level, and ability to understand English, so the communication program must consider these factors.

A multimedia approach to participant communications works best, because people absorb different kinds of information best from different media. For example, a video might work best for presenting a new plan and its benefits, whereas supporting print materials would provide more details on the plan's investment options. Further, some cultures respond better to live presentations as opposed to print material, which is an important consideration for multicultural workforces.

All participant communications materials must be created and delivered with an intended goal. Whether the objective is to increase participation, improve diversification, or simply introduce new investment options, the message must be clear in order to have significant impact on participants.

A plan consultant or financial advisor is an excellent resource for assistance with participant communications because these individuals make their living explaining difficult investing concepts in layperson's terms.

# UNDERSTANDING FEES IN 401(k) PLANS

Cost is a major factor in selecting a service provider, and perhaps the most important point here is to have a clear sense of each candidate's fee structure so they may be a meaningful comparison. Service providers all have different fee structures and different ways of representing them, depending on the level of service included in a package. As such, plan sponsors may find the fee review confusing and should take advantage of their plan consultant's expertise to clarify issues in this area.

Given the variety of service packages available and the range of fee structures presented by service providers, there is little meaningful research on average costs in 401(k) plan service arrangements, and plan sponsors can be more knowledgeable buyers by at least knowing for what to look.

It is critical that all expenses be weighed carefully against the performance of a provider's investment options, because investment performance in mutual funds is meaningless unless it occurs in the context of performance. Conversely, investment performance in separately managed accounts may not be net of all expenses. In either event, plan sponsors may find that although a provider may look expensive in comparison to others, attractive fund performance can compensate for higher costs and make the provider a more attractive candidate.

Sponsors should carefully review each cost item with a plan consultant, and it is important to recognize, at a minimum, the following cost items:

- Investment management fees represent the actual cost for portfolio management services and are usually based on a percentage of a plan's assets under management. In many cases investment management fees do not include internal operating expenses and transactional costs for mutual funds, so it is important to look for these costs as separate items.

- Internal operating expenses refer to legal fees, fund accounting, transfer agent fees, and 12b(1) fees, among others, for mutual funds and insurance company investments. These internal fund-operating expenses can vary significantly depending on the fund group and the size of the fund.

- Contract administration charges, unique to insurance company separate accounts, vary depending on the carrier and may be either an annual percentage charge or hard-dollar fee. Plan sponsors should ask the carrier what services this fee covers.

- Trust fees, although not an investment cost, are usually applied against the assets of the plan and can be fixed-dollar amounts or an asset-based percentage.

- Investment consultant fees cover the cost of having a consultant or advisor help the plan manage fiduciary responsibilities relating to investment management and employee communications. These charges may be either fixed-dollar amounts or asset-based fees and should be considered part of the total cost to manage the plan's assets.

- Participant communications fees vary depending on the method of this service delivery. Most large service providers include some level of employee communications in their bundled package but may have additional feed for more elaborate communications programs. Participant communications provided by the plan consultant may require separate charges altogether.

# SUMMARY

The most fruitful service provider search will result in the best package of services at the best possible price given a particular plan's size and unique requirements. The good news is that the 401(k) plan market place has evolved to such an extent that there are suitable service arrangements available for virtually any 401(k) plan. Plan sponsors will service themselves and their participants well by taking the time to understand the administrative and regulatory issues that impact their plans along with the unique needs of their participants. This market continues to evolve, bringing new products and services along with new concerns and challenges. As such, plan sponsors need the support of outside experts to help them become not simply knowledgeable buyers but the most effective 401(k) plan managers.

Printed in the United States
67577LVS00004B/137